Homestyle
MIDDLE EASTERN
Cooking

Homestyle MIDDLE EASTERN Cooking

by
PAT CHAPMAN

THE CROSSING PRESS
FREEDOM, CALIFORNIA

Published in 1997 in the U.S.A. by The Crossing Press
© 1989 Pat Chapman
First published in the U.K. in 1989 by
Judy Piatkus (Publishers) Ltd.

Cover design by Victoria May
Edited by Susan Fleming
Photography by Tim Imrie
Illustrated by Zena Flax and Hanife Hassan
Map on page 7 by Dick Vine

For information on bulk purchases or group discounts for this and other Crossing Press titles, please contact our Special Sales Manager at 800-777-1048.

ISBN-0-89594-860-5

CONTENTS

INTRODUCTION

Middle Eastern cuisine has its roots thousands of years ago, at the very beginning of civilization. Bread-making, wine-making, brewing, yogurt, kebabs, and probably cooking itself originated there, yet I suspect that a great many of us born and living in the "West" know relatively little about the food of the Middle East. Its image is sometimes off-putting—of arid deserts and scarcity of water, of millennia of a "waste-not-want-not" lifestyle. Bedouins eat sheep's eyes, lizards, locusts' and camels' testicles, hooves, tails, and tongues. These may be delicacies to Bedouin tribes, but not the normal everyday fare enjoyed in the West. Middle Eastern food is wholesome, varied, and delicious. Nutritionally, it makes best use of the enormous range of produce in the area: fresh fruit and vegetables, meat, poultry and fish, nuts, grain and dairy produce, spices and herbs, which are readily available and they are prepared in innumerable and delicious ways.

You'd be forgiven for believing that Middle Eastern food consists only of hummus, taramasalata, doner kebabs, shish kebabs, roast meat or poultry, rice, pita bread, yogurt, fruity desserts, thick coffee, and Turkish Delight. All these items do exist, of course. I love them all, and recipes for them appear in this book. They have their rightful place in the Middle Eastern repertoire, but, as you might suspect, they are only the tip of an enormous, edible, Middle Eastern iceberg of culinary delights.

What is meant by the term "Middle East"? Technically, there are fourteen countries defined on the map on page 7: Syria, Lebanon, Jordan, Iraq, Iran, Egypt, Saudi Arabia, and the Gulf States of the United Arab Emirates. They have in common the Arabic language, Islamic religion, thousands of years of history and culture, and cuisine. When I first started to think about writing a Middle Eastern cookbook, I thought that I would confine myself to these fourteen countries. However, as any visitor to the North African Mediterranean countries knows, the people there also have a way of life and a cuisine which, though it has a lot in common with their Middle Eastern neighbors, has a lot of dishes and cooking methods that are unique to the area, Moroccan food in particular being absolutely superb. Therefore, I have included recipes from the four Maghreb countries of Morocco, Algeria, Tunisia, and Libya.

To the immediate north of the Middle East lies Turkey. Straddling Europe and Asia, Turkey has its own language and culture, and while it is not considered a part of the recognized Middle East, it has always had deep roots in the Arab-Islamic world and vice versa.

Turkish food was largely developed by the Ottoman emperors, and though it is distinctively different from that of the Middle East, it has had a tremendous influence on that cuisine. I could not omit it from this book. At its height, the Ottoman Empire ruled Greece and Cyprus with cross-fertilization of culinary ideas occurring between these three countries, so I have included a few Greek recipes and a Cypriot recipe.

There are three other places, each once a kingdom in its own right, which over the millennia have played their part in shaping the cuisine of the Middle East. Known as Armenia, Azerbaijan, and Georgia, they are now semi-independent republics of the former Soviet Union. Their influence on Middle Eastern cuisine cannot be ignored, and I have included a number of recipes from each of these regions.

Finally, there is Israel. The food there is fundamentally Arabic, but has been changed over the last four decades by the innovations and traditions of its new immigrants.

So there we have it: a total of twenty-five countries in three continents, Africa, Europe, and Asia; 227 million people speaking many languages and of several creeds; people with fundamental differences, but with much in common. And perhaps the greatest thing they have in common is food.

Over the years I have visited many of these twenty-five countries. I have been able to amass a huge collection of information and recipes. Though I have concentrated largely on traditional Middle Eastern cooking, with many of the recipes originating in antiquity, I must make the point that every single dish is contemporary, eaten and relished by today's Middle Eastern people.

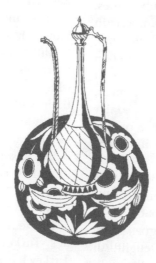

CULINARY BACKGROUND

Before we get down to the business of the recipes, I'd like to give you some insight into the Middle East. There are twenty-five countries grouped together for the purpose of this book; some are at war with their neighbors and have little in common except hatred; others are thousands of miles apart, but are close politically. Some are in what was formerly Russia, some in Europe, some in Africa, and most in Asia. Each has a fascinating past which goes back to the beginnings of civilization with a common history.

So join me on a journey over 12,000 years and 10,000 miles as we meet the 230 million people of the Middle East, their twenty-five countries, and above all, their wonderful food.

THE MAGHREBI: MOROCCO, ALGERIA, TUNISIA AND LIBYA

Many of us were first introduced to the Arabic way of life when we took a holiday in Morocco or Tunisia. Those who venture out of their tourist cocoon into the ancient towns find that little has changed over the centuries. They see a largely peasant population whose language, religion, and existence are influenced by 1,000 years of Arab rule.

Centuries ago, Morocco, Algeria, and Tunisia formed one country known as the Maghrebi, the land of the setting sun or the land at the end of the world. In those days the Atlantic Ocean was the verge of a flat world beyond which it was believed that mariners who proceeded would fall off. The original inhabitants of the area were the nomadic, primitive Berbers. Still nomadic, fierce, pale-skinned and blue-eyed, the Berbers found in Morocco are easily distinguished by their long brown and white robes with peaked hoods.

From about A.D. 700, a succession of Arab conquerors ruled the Maghrebi, bringing in their culture and the religion of Islam. Little changed until power shifted to the Turkish Ottoman Empire in 1535. By 1715 the Ottomans relinquished control, and Libya, under the name of Tripoli, was created. The departure of the Ottomans eventually allowed European colonizers to move in and take possession of the various lands of the Maghrebi: Spain in Morocco, France in Algeria and Tunisia, and Italy in Libya. Independence finally came to Libya in 1951, Tunisia and Morocco in1956, and Algeria in 1962.

The cooking of the four Maghrebi countries has strong Arab and Ottoman roots and even a Persian influence, yet it has a unique style, resulting from the continuous presence of the Berbers. Invaders such as the Carthaginians also influenced Maghrebi cuisine. They used the Maghrebi coasts as trading posts in the centuries before Christ and probably intro-duced durum wheat flour. They also intro-duced the process of making semolina. From this decidedly Italian food, the Berbers invented the Maghrebi's most celebrated dish, couscous. It consists of small grains of semolina which are steamed over a pot of meat, poultry, or vegetable broth.

Of the four Maghrebi countries, Libyan cooking perhaps shows the most obvious Arab influence. It has also been influenced by Italy, but Italian cuisine does not play a large part in contemporary Libya, where poverty is prevalent. Nevertheless, Libya has some excellent dishes which I have included in this book (see pages 46, 52, 102 and 142).

Tunisian food has been influenced by Italian cuisine, with pasta and tomatoes appearing frequently. Tunisians also adore extremely hot food. Their red chile paste, harissa, appears on the table at all meals including breakfast.

Algerian cooking has been very strongly influenced recently by the French. Very little spice is used in Algerian food. The Algerian *chakchouka* (ratatouille) should not be missed.

Moroccan cooking stands out as one of the best, not only of the Maghrebi, but of the whole Middle East. It is complex and varied, delicious, and full of surprises. It has taken the best of the Arab and Turkish repertoires, added a uniqueness of its own, and undoubt-edly gained from the more recent French influences. Moroccan cooking uses spices effectively, and in some cases liberally. It uses the world's most extraordinary spice mixture, *ras-el-hanout*, in some dishes. Sometimes a single spice (cumin is very popular) is all that is called for. The spicy paste *chermoula* is a par-ticularly popular marinade, used with fish, meat, and poultry which is then spit-roasted, sometimes stuffed, or is glazed with spices, nuts, and honey.

Many Moroccan dishes require a special pastry called *warkha*, similar to filo and which requires years of practice and skill to make. I have stood for hours watching it being done in a Tangiers bakery. The best *warkha* should be rolled thinner than tracing paper. *Briouats* (called *breiks* in Tunisia and *boureks* in Algeria) are small pastries made from *warkha* stuffed with various fillings. But the *warkha* which is often regarded as Morocco's real masterpiece is *bisteeya*, a pie containing ground pigeon, nuts, dried fruit, scrambled eggs and spices, and seasoned with confectioner's sugar and lemon juice. This intriguing mixture of savory, sweet, and sour, so typically Persian in origin, appears elsewhere in the Maghrebi. I must allow myself the memory of drooling on many occasions at a Moroccan bakery, trying to decide whether to invest in *m'hancha*—the snake cake made from *warkha* pastry stuffed with almond paste, rolled into a tight sausage, coiled into a Catherine wheel, baked, and then sprinkled with confectioner's sugar, with a lattice of ground cinnamon—or perhaps a *shebbakia*, curly pastry ribbons, deep-fried, then soaked in honey, and sprinkled with sesame seeds, or indeed a dozen other aston-ishing pastry delights, all accompanied by that great Moroccan experience, mint tea or *naa'naa*.

EGYPT

Of all the countries of the Middle East, none has a more colorful past than Egypt. The original inhabitants, the Hamites, inhabited Egypt by 4500 B.C. There they took advantage of the highly fertile delta of the Nile, the world's longest river, to establish a civiliza-tion. By 2900 B.C., the world's first kingdom was established, and the Pharaohs were to rule virtually uninterrupted for nearly 3,000 years, an achievement unequaled by any other civiliztion. The Pharaohs eventually succumbed to the Romans in 30 B.C., then later it (Egypt) fell to the Moslem Arabs by 642 A.D. It remained under a succession of caliphates and sultanates for nearly 900 years, until taken over by the Ottoman Turks in 1517. Ottoman power began to wane in the late nineteenth century. Napoleon Bonaparte imposed French influence in Egypt in 1798, resulting in the opening of the French-conceived Suez Canal in 1869. In 1947 Egypt achieved independence. Although the greater part of the Egyptian population is now Moslem, there is a strong Christian community, the Copts, who claim to be direct descendants of the early Egyptians.

The Egyptians adore certain spices, such as cumin which they export worldwide and garlic. However, they do not relish the heat of hot chiles. Bean and lentil dishes are popular. Egyptians are prolific egg eaters; in Pharaonic days they operated egg hatcheries with incubators. Poultry is equally popular, as well as goose liver, quail, and pigeon.

ISRAEL

Currently, Israel has a population of 3.5 million. Few Israelis are native. Most Israelis were Jews who had lived in Europe who returned to Israel after its formation in 1948, bringing a modern outlook and technology to a very barren land. Irrigation and agriculture have produced fertile farm lands on which grow superb quality vegetables and fruit. Adroit marketing has made Israeli oranges, capsicum peppers, avocados, melons, okra, and zucchini available in markets throughout Europe. Geese are also reared in quantity for export to France, specifically for the manufacture of pâté de foie gras.

Many Israeli dishes are familiar wherever there are Jewish communities in the world. Some dishes are similar, if not identical, to those of their Arab neighbors. Falafel, for example, is regarded as an Israeli national dish.

There are some superb dishes unique to Israel. Latkes, for example, are pancakes made from grated potatoes, eggs, and onions. Because Jews may not cook on Saturday, the Sabbath, *cholent*, a spiced stew of meat and vegetables, is started on Friday evening and baked all night so that it is still hot at dinner. *Gefilte* (fish balls) and bagels are other well-known Israeli foods. One modern dish from Israel is *sabra* dip, made from avocados. Israeli desserts include *blintzes*, a sweet or savory rolled pancake filled either with curd cheese and dates, or a ground meat and gravy.

THE LEVANT: JORDAN, PALESTINE, LEBANON, SYRIA, AND IRAQ

In the fertile crescent created by the Euphrates and Tigris Rivers man first became "civilized." Some 12,000 years ago he learned to farm, to domesticate himself and his animals, to build cities, and to trade. Later it became the granary of the Roman Empire. The Arabs took possession of the region from A.D. 700 to the fifteenth century. The Ottomans ruled from the fifteenth century until the end of World War I when Palestine, Lebanon, Syria, and Iraq emerged as independent states.

Unlike its neighbors, Lebanon has a highly sophisticated restaurant tradition influenced by the French colonists. Beirut was a fashionable tourist resort of great beauty, and I well remember its curving bay, yachts, and sunsets, its wealth and its restaurants. Today only the sunsets and the memories remain. Many Lebanese restaurateurs fled the country to set up new ventures in new continents. Consequently, when we think of Middle Eastern food these days, it is Lebanese food we are remembering. But it is true that the food of the Levant countries is very similar to that found in Lebanon.

One of the most celebrated range of dishes is the mezzeh. Famous all over the Middle East, these appetizers and finger foods are especially excellent in the Levant. I describe them in more detail in Chapter Four. They range from simple dishes of olives, nuts, or salads to complex dips, cooked items, and pastries. Mezzehs are always accompanied by breads such as *kaak* or *khubiz sorj* from the Lebanon, and *sh'raak* in Jordan and Palestine. Another type of bread is *kaark*, a crisp sesame-coated "bracelet." Often mezzehs are so satisfying, so numerous, and so filling that they become a meal in themselves. But you must find room for the fabulous main courses, of which *kibbeh* is probably regarded as the national dish. It is a mixture of spicy ground lamb and cracked wheat. Spicy meat dishes are also popular. Another popular dish is lamb cooked in yogurt (*labnah ummo*), called *mansi* in Palestine.

There is a wide range of vegetable dishes to choose from including the classic *kibbeh*-stuffed zucchini (*kossa mashiya*), stir-fried okra (*bamiya*) and white haricot beans (*fassoolia baydah*) from Syria. A particularly interesting dish is *roz bi sha'riya*, which combines rice and vermicelli. And if all that was not enough—enter the dessert tray. Syrupy, honey-laced, nutty pastries such as baklava and *kadayif* cannot be resisted.

THE GULF: SAUDI ARABIA, YEMEN, OMAN, QATAR, KUWAIT, BAHRAIN, THE UNITED ARAB EMIRATES

The Arabian peninsula is a region of arid wastelands and deserts, punctuated by occasional water wells or oases. For thousands of years it was home to indigenous tribes who were able to crisscross those wastelands and survive. This traveling presented Arabs with the opportunity to act as traders between the Mediterranean countries and India. They had nothing of their own to trade, but, acting as middlemen, they became extremely wealthy, and with wealth came power. Eventually, in the name of their newfound religion—

Islam—they used their wealth and power to become empire builders.

The Prophet Mohammed was born in the late sixth century (ca. 570 A.D.). He was forty years old when he founded the Islamic religion, which led to the expansion of the Arab territories in the name of Allah. His followers took Damascus, then captured the Sind (Pakistan), went on to India, and later entered China. They took all the territories of the southern Mediterranean and Spain and they went on to occupy southern France until they were finally driven out in 732. By 900 A.D. when their empire was at its height they captured Baghdad.

The Empire of the Moors lasted for seven centuries, until it was replaced by a regime it had created—the Moslem Ottoman Turks. Arab power waned exactly at the time when their importance as spice traders was supplanted by northern European mariners. Arabia retreated to its peninsula, to insignificance, to poverty, and to the old nomadic ways of the Bedouin tribes. Then in the middle of this century, the hand of fortune caressed Arabia once again. This time it was with oil, and with it has come a rapid and profound change of lifestyle. Bedouin tribes still dwell in the deserts of the Gulf, but today one is more likely to encounter Coca-Cola and Suzukis than camels.

New wealth and high speed communication have brought burger and pizza bars, luxury hotels, and restaurants within reach of all but the most distant townships. Despite this Western onslaught, traditional Arab food is excellent, benefiting from their foreign trade and conquests. Popular Arab spices include the bitter fenugreek (typified in the dip *hilbeh*). Garlic and chiles are also enjoyed. Because of their direct link to India, the southern states of the Gulf produce spicy dishes, some very hot. *Kiymeh mashwi*, for example, is a curried mince dish from Oman, derived from the Indian *keema*. *Kofta* (meat balls in spicy gravy) is another dish with an Indo-Persian background. Other Gulf meat and poultry dishes include *kirshuh* (spicy Yemeni offal stir-fry), *djej mechoui* (roast chicken), and *dajaj m'ashi* (stuffed chicken). *Blehal samak* are fish fingers, and *nachbous* is a spicy Kuwaiti prawn stir-fry. Vegetable dishes include *karafsi magaah* (sautéed celery), *korrat bi zayt* (sautéed leeks), and *sheik-el-ma'sh* (zucchini stuffed with ground meat). *Timman* is Iraqi fried rice, and *khoubiz* is the standard, the round bread found in one form or another in every country mentioned in this book.

The Arabs have a definite sweet tooth and enjoy the sticky honey-dripping pastries like *baklava* and *kunafa*. It is the date, indigenous to the Gulf, which Arabs eat all day and every day in every guise conceivable. *Q'ahwah*, Arab coffee, is also consumed spiced or plain, usually very sweet, and always very strong. Twenty cups a day is the norm to the average Arab.

But I have left Arabia's most famous dish until last—*khouzi* (whole roast lamb), and its simpler variation, *fakhid kharouf* (roast leg of lamb).

IRAN (PERSIA)

Is it Persia or is it Iran? To find out we must go back over 30,000 years. As the last glacier receded northwards over Europe and Asia, a race of people known as Indo-Europeans evolved in the area north of the Caucasian mountains (between the Black Sea and the Caspian mountains). As their population expanded, these nomadic tribes branched out, eventually occupying much of Europe, thus becoming the direct ancestors of most modern Europeans. Other branches moved eastward and by 3000 B.C. they had settled in the plains of Turkestan, north of Afghanistan. These tribes were called Aryans, and by now they had become cattle herders and dairy farmers. They also invented the horse-drawn chariot, a weapon which gave them easy victory in their conquests. By 2300 B.C., another branch of the tribes, the Parsi-Aryans, entered this land. At first it was called Iran, a derivative of the word "Aryans." Later the land was called Parthia or Persia, a derivative of the word "parsi." Over the next 1,500 years the Iranians settled into their land. They perfected the technique of dairy production. What has endured from these times is the Aryan tradition of cooking with dairy products, especially yogurt, fundamental to contemporary Indian, Caucasian, and Iranian cooking.

In 646 B.C. the Persian King of the Medes defeated the neighboring Assyrians and established the first Persian Empire. It lasted until the arrival of Alexander the Great in 323 B.C. The Persian Empire made a comeback as Alexander's Greece declined. Between A.D. 145 and A.D. 626 it existed alongside Rome, during which time the Persian style of cooking developed to great heights.

Then came the Arabs and with them Islam. The Persians readily became Moslems, and the Arabs took to Persian cooking, exporting it to all parts of their expanding empire. Persian monarchs continued to rule the same way they did when the Arabs were ousted by the Ottomans in the fifteenth century. Indeed it was dissatisfaction with generations of autocratic rulers which led to the deposition of the Shah in 1979. It was then that the country was renamed Iran.

Persian food has evolved over very many centuries. It has a very distinctive style. Many dishes combine unlikely ingredients of sweet, sour, and savory tastes. For example, meat marinated in yogurt is slowly simmered in pomegranate juice with spices, molasses, honey (or sugar), and lemon. Whole almonds or pistachio nuts are added. Cooked apricots, peaches, prunes, dates, or apples often accompany this dish. Spicing can be quite

5

subtle or can predominate. Derivatives of the Persian style are found as far away as Morocco, in *bisteeya* for example, Tunisia *mishmisheya*, and in Turkey *tavak koftesi*. Variations of the *kofta* meatball dish are favorites in most Arab countries and in India, imported there by the Persian and Arab invaders.

The art of rice cooking almost certainly began in Persia. *Pollou* gave birth to the many similar Middle Eastern rice dishes, *chellow* and *tahig*. *Nane lavash* is a thin, floppy Iranian bread, while *lavash* is very crisp.

TURKEY

The earliest civilized settlers in Anatolia (Turkey) were a tribe called the Hittites, who were established there by 2500 B.C. By 480 B.C. the area had become part of the enormous Persian Empire. This fell to Greece by 323 B.C. Later, Anatolia became Christian, and Constantinople (now Istanbul) grew to be a major Roman trading center. As the Roman Empire declined it divided into two, and in A.D. 629 the eastern division became Byzantium. In 1071 it fell to Moslems who invaded from the Levant.

THE CULINARY COUNTRIES OF THE MIDDLE EAST

The countries of our culinary Middle East spread a total of 4,200 miles from west (Morocco) to east (Iran) and 2,200 miles north (Turkey) to the south (Yemen). It has a total area of 4.6 million square miles, and a population of 227 million. (The USA, by comparison, spans some 3,000 miles by 1,600 miles, has an area of 3.6 million square miles and a population of 200 million.) In terms of longitude, the span is 13°W to 63°E and latitude 10°N to 43°N with most of the landmasses located at around 30°. It is hot, and much of the land is very arid.

Some Statistics

Languages. Arabic is spoken by 11 million people in seventeen of the countries. Other languages include Turkish (50 million), Persian (43 million), Russian (14 million), Greek (10 million) and Hebrew (2 million).

Religions. Islam is the religion of over 200 million of the people. Christianity is the principal religion of Greece and Cyprus and is widespread in Georgia, Lebanon and Armenia. Judaism is the principal religion in Israel.

The original Turks were descendants of the ancient Aryan tribes, inhabiting the area of the former Soviet Union that is still called Turkestan. By A.D. 550 they became powerful enough to control a kingdom. Over the next 500 years their power base extended, and they eventually became Moslem.

By 1400, it was the Turkish Ottomans who controlled eastern Greece and Turkey. That empire continued to expand over the next 400 years until they controlled all the countries discussed in this book with the exception of Morocco and Persia. The beginning of this century saw the Ottoman Empire still intact but suffering from a feudal sultanate wracked with indecision, corruption, and mistakes, finally epitomized by its leaders (for no good reason) siding with the losers of World War I. The outcome was the dismantling of their empire in 1919, its territories divided between Britain and France. The country was named Turkey for the first time. (Throughout the Ottoman period the word "Turk" was synonymous with "barbarian tribesman," a deep insult.) A series of major cultural reforms was enforced, and the government was secularized, the Arabic script was abolished, and the Roman alphabet was adopted. Most Turks are Moslem but do not strictly adhere to Islam's tenets.

THE CULINARY COUNTRIES OF THE MIDDLE EAST

The countries of our culinary Middle East spread a total of 4,200 miles (6,720 km) from the west (Morocco) to east (Iran) and 2,200 miles (3,520 km) north (Turkey) to south (Yemen). It has a total area of 4.6 million square miles, and a population of 227 million. (The USA, by comparison, spans some 3,000 miles by 1,600 miles, has an area of 3.6 million square miles and a population of 200 million.) In terms of longitude the span is 13°W to 63°E and latitude of 10°N to 43°S with most of the landmasses being located at around 30°. Climatically therefore, it it hot, and much of the land is very arid desert.

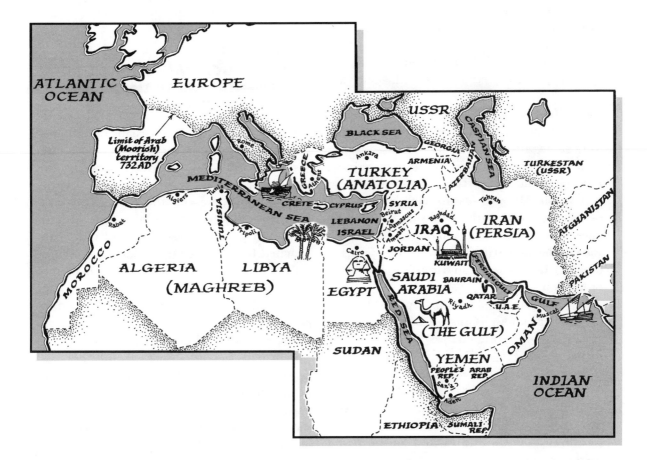

SOME STATISTICS

Languages. Arabic is spoken by 11 million people in seventeen of the countries. Others include Turkish (50 million), Persian (43 million), Russian (14 million), and Greek (10 million) and Hebrew (2 million).

Religion. Islam is the religion of over 200 million of the people. Christianity is the principal religion of Greece and Cyprus and it is widespread in Georgia, the Lebanon and Armenia. Judaism is the principal religion in Israel.

The powerful and long-lived Ottoman Empire was one of the world's most colorful, brutal, and despotic regimes. Its sultans enjoyed all the comforts that their wealth and power could afford. Their palaces glittered with gold and jewels, and their harems and belly dancers were renowned. But perhaps their greatest legacy is their food, arguably the best and most imaginative of all the countries in this book, even surpassing (but only just) that of Morocco. The names of some of the dishes themselves indicate what was on the sultans' minds, when their chefs created them for their masters. Dishes such as "Ladies' Navels," "Ladies' Thighs," "Sweet Lips," "Dainty Fingers" and "Turkish Delight" regularly appeared at court and are still Turkish favorites.

Entertaining at home, instead of at restaurants, is traditional in Turkey and sometimes very lavish. Mezzehs feature largely on such occasions, and the array of dishes is virtually endless. Even the table on which these are served, the "Raki (the locally produced anise liqueur) table," sums up Turkish enjoyment of mezzeh.

Taramasalata, a fish roe dip, is probably one of the best-known Greek/Turkish mezzeh dishes. Other representative Turkish dishes include *kiymail yumarta* (ground meat topped with egg), *kestaneli hindi guveci* (turkey casserole with chestnuts) and *pilich dolmesi* (boned, stuffed chicken). There is a wealth of fish dishes including *kilich shish* (skewered swordfish). *Sardalya* and *hamsi tavasi* are pan-fried sardines and anchovies respectively, and *baliklar koftesi* are fish balls. *Istakoz firinda* is a baked lobster dish, and there are dozens of vegetable dishes of unsurpassed quality.

Khave turki (Turkish coffee), as with all the Arab nations, is a way of life with the Turks. Tiny cups of very thick strong coffee are drunk at any time of the day, usually black, and frequently with a lot of sugar. Even more popular than coffee is *chaiy turki* (Turkish tea), which is also readily available. Street vendors carry polished brass "back-pack" urns to dispense coffee or tea to paying passersby. A similar urn, made of glass, dispenses *visine*, a sour cherry drink or lemonade.

Finally, mention must be made of that world-famous confectionery, *lokum*, better known as Turkish Delight. Naturally pale in color, it is made from grape pulp, semolina, and gelatin, with icing sugar sprinkled on top after it is set.

THE CAUCASIAN COUNTRIES: ARMENIA, AZERBAIJAN, AND GEORGIA

Geographically, the Caucasian mountains, which stretch from the Black Sea to the Caspian, form a natural divide. To the south, lie Turkey and Iran and the Pontic mountains. (It was on the highest peak of these mountains, the 17,000-foot Mount Ararat, that the Old Testament tells us Noah beached his Ark after the Flood.) A sub-race called the Caucasians evolved north of the mountains and by 4500 B.C. they had expanded to occupy the Levant, Turkey, and parts of Greece and Iran. Later they were pushed back to their original homelands, which had become part of the Persian Empire by 646 B.C. After a series of wars, the Kingdom of Armenia was established, and in A.D. 303 it became the world's first Christian state, preceding Rome by 34 years. With the decline of the Roman Empire, Armenia was absorbed into the expanding Persian Empire. It reemerged as an independent kingdom by A.D. 650, but fell victim to Arab ascendancy in 717. Armenia and Azerbaijan, under Moslem Emirs, turned largely to Islam, but the tiny kingdom of Abasgia (later called Georgia), remained the sole center of the Eastern Church despite becoming a part of the Russian Empire in 1783.

In culinary terms the food is a combination of Arab and Turkish styles. Though it is not impossible today to visit the often war-torn Republics of Armenia, Azerbaijan, and Georgia, it is more likely that one will encounter their food in the few restaurants run by Armenian emigrés in the West. My recipe selection includes the outstanding poultry dish *cerkez tavagu* (chicken cooked in a paste of paprika, walnuts, garlic, and oil), which is regarded as the national dish. *Uskumru plaki* is mackerel casserole, *bras yahni* a dish of sautéed leeks. Chickpeas make their appearance in *nivig* (with spinach), served cold during Lent.

Highly specialized items, such as the dried meats and sausages of these regions, are best left to the professionals, as they require skill and the hot sun. However, they are often obtainable at specialty delicatessens and Middle Eastern markets in many American cities. *Aboukht* is beef, seasoned with salt and a fenugreek paste, dried in the sun. It is called pastrami in neighboring Soviet countries and *pastrouma* in Greece, Turkey, and Israel. *Mortadella* is a spicy lamb or mutton sausage which is used in the Armenian pastas *rishata* and *arshta*. With its Aryan and Persian links, *mazdoon* (yogurt) is widely used, particularly in the yogurt drink *tam*, which is similar to *abdug*.

GREECE AND CYPRUS

Historically, Greece is probably best remembered for its ancient empire which, by 323 B.C., was at its height under Alexander the Great, claiming territory from India to Spain. That empire gave way to Rome, and later, by A.D. 650, Greece was partly in the hands of Byzantium, Rome's eastern replacement, while central Greece fell into the hands of a tribe called the Avar Huns, later known as the Bulgars. By 1000, the Byzantines had recovered most of Greece and Turkey; but they were gradually to lose Turkey and retreat back into Greece. By 1453, Byzantium had finally crumbled and Greece was incorporated into the Turkish Ottoman Empire. It was not until the nineteenth century that the kingdom of Greece was established in the south of the country, and by 1912 it had taken back all of Greece from Turkey, establishing Greece once again in Europe. Centuries of Arab-Turkish culture and Islam were finally expelled in favor of Christianity. Politically, enmity remains to this day, highlighted in the divided island of Cyprus.

Although modern Greece is not part of the Middle East, its links over the centuries are too strong to ignore. At first I had decided to omit Greek and Cypriot recipes because so many of their dishes owe their origins to Turkey. But it is not quite as simple as that. Certain dishes originated long before the Turkish Moslem occupation and are directly attributable to Byzantine influences. Certain other Greek dishes owe their origins to the Turkish Ottomans. As a general rule, Greek dishes are mellower than Turkish ones, with spices used but to a lesser extent. The many dishes which share names, such as *mezzeh* (itself derived from a Greek word), *dolmas* (stuffed items), *pilafis* (rice dishes), the savory and sweet *filo* (stuffed pastry items), the use of yogurt (*jiarouru*) and the strong, thick, sweet coffee will be found not only in Greece and Turkey, but in much of the Arab world in one form or another. I have decided to omit most recipes that are found only in Greece.

Three Greek dishes that I have included because they are so delicious are *spanokopita*, little filo pastry pies with spinach and feta cheese, and its two variations, *tyropita* and *kotopita*, the first with egg and cheese filling and the second with ground chicken.

TOWN LIFE

The Arab town and city is a vibrant, colorful hive of bustle, noise, and social encounter. People scurry from place to place about their business, or sit in laughing, talkative groups at street cafés, relaxing over endless cups of coffee and tidbits—the women apart from the men.

In the Arab heartlands, dress is almost wholly traditional—the men in white or colored robes and elegant headdresses, the women always in *yashmaks*, often in black. The sun beats down, the streets are none too clean, the smells mingle, some pleasant, some not. Motor vehicles clatter past, horns shrieking endlessly; donkeys, camels, mules, and bullocks piled high with wares plod wearily by; lean cats and dogs seek scraps and exotic birds flash from pole to pole.

No matter how large and modern the city, it always has its market or *soukh, cazbah,* or *medina.* Whether the city is Cairo or Tangiers, Istanbul or Jeddah, Baghdad or Tehran, it is usually walled and very ancient, and inside it is like going back in time. Motor vehicles are usually not permitted into the maze of twisting lanes between the tall buildings. But it is the many traders who form the main interest in the *soukh.* Nothing has changed for centuries. It is a place for buying and selling and every conceivable commodity can be found there: pots, pans, clothing, perfume, ornaments, jewelry, flowers, livestock, fish, meat, vegetables, groceries, freshly baked bread, yogurt, cheese, and milk. Between the shops and stalls and handcarts, there are traders who have staked out a small place to stand or sit. Often there is precious little on sale. One man may be trying to sell one scrawny goat, another a few saucepans. A heavily veiled woman may have a few freshly picked carrots for sale and another may be selling yogurt in earthenware pots. These people come in from their villages from time

to time in order to earn their keep for a few days. People shout and haggle, traders call out their wares, and money and goods change hands in a ritual as old as civilization itself.

RELIGION AND DIETARY TABOOS

The world's oldest monotheistic religion—Judaism—evolved in the Middle East as early as 2000 B.C., with the establishment of Abraham's wandering tribe. The formalized growth of Judaism did not take place until around 800 B.C., some 300 years after the establishment of Israel (the Old Testament was not written until around 300 B.C.). Judaism, the basis of Christianity and Islam, is practiced today by about 12 million people, half of whom are living in the U.S. and 4 million in Israel.

Christianity also originated in Israel and there are some 25 million Christians living in the Middle East. The first converts to Christianity were the Egyptians: today's descendants, who can trace their ancestry back to Pharaonic times, are the Coptic Christians. The Armenians were converted in A.D. 303, the Romans followed in 337, then the Turks and Greeks. The people of these nations, with the exception of the modern Italians, belong to the Eastern Orthodox faith, with its center in Istanbul. There is also a small pocket of Christianity in Lebanon.

The third religion to come out of the Middle East was Islam, Arabia being its birthplace. Of the 227 million people in the Middle East, 87 percent are Moslem.

Both Judaism and Islam have certain taboos about food. Orthodox Jews eat only food which is kosher, which means fit and proper, and Moslems eat only food which is halal, or clean. Failure to keep these laws is unthinkable to fundamentalists of both religions. Kosher and halal foods must be prepared and eaten according to unbreakable rules. Meat must be slaughtered, cut in a particular way, and blood must not be present in the meat ready for cooking. Pork is prohibited in both religions. Jews may not eat invertebrates such as shellfish and snails, although this does not apply to Moslems. Jews may not cook on Saturdays, their Sabbath, but they may eat on that day. Moslems may not eat between sunup and sundown during their month-long fast of Ramadan. Moslems still practice ritual sacrifice (e.g., of a lamb or kid), Christians must practice abstention during their month-long period of Lent. Christians are prohibited from eating red meat on Fridays, in memory of the Crucifixion.

COOKING METHODS AND UTENSILS

Most of the population of the Middle East live in primitive conditions. Running water, gas, or electricity are found only in the largest villages. The average Western kitchen, with its efficient work surfaces, its oven and stove, hot and cold running water, freezer, refrigerator, dishwasher, food processor, blender, and microwave, would seem like a spaceship to all but the wealthiest Middle Eastern peoples. Even in the larger cities, the middle class does not possess more than the most basic modern conveniences but, despite this, any Middle Eastern cook seems to be able to produce magnificent fare from the most limited resources.

Most homes still rely on a single burner, often a kerosene burner, though many use their hearth or a simple charcoal or wood fire instead. Timing and technique enable the cook to prepare several dishes at the same time on the single heat source. The local bakery (*furunji*) in the Middle East not only has bread to sell, but the charcoal-fired ovens can be used by the local people for other matters. Rather like taking one's wash to the laundromat, the cook simply takes her dish to the *furun* (baker), who, for a few

pennies, will bake stews, turning, stirring, and even adding any ingredients supplied, or he will bake cakes, pastries, or bread made from the customer's own dough. The customer can either return for the finished work at an agreed time, or may wait at the bakery enjoying the company of friends over cups of coffee. The *furunji* is not just a practical necessity, it is an enjoyable meeting place and focal point for social interaction, especially for women.

The Middle Eastern cook uses a round baking dish called *tapsi* in Greece and *sanieh* in Arabic, and a lidded casserole dish, *tsoukali*. Other utensils include pottery dishes, copper pans (now giving way to aluminum), and a cast iron or steel frying pan, usually shaped like a wok. Every cook has a mortar and pestle, and a special, long-handled pot to make the ubiquitous Arab coffee. There is a wicker or woven basket through which to strain yogurt, and for specialty dishes there are utensils to match the need. The Egyptian bean dish, *ful medames,* requires a double boiler, in the cylindrical, tapering top of which the beans slowly cook. North African couscous is cooked in a pan with a different shape but similar concept, called the *couscousière,* and there are special rice cookers. None of this need daunt the Western cook, who will be perfectly able to prepare and cook any of the recipes in this book without special equipment.

MEALS OF THE DAY

Most Middle Eastern people eat three meals a day with breakfast traditionally lighter than lunch and dinner. A typical breakfast might include *labnah* (yogurt cheese) spiced with *za'atar,* a blend of powdered herbs. Olives and dates, plain or stuffed, and fresh fruit, honey, and nuts are usually present. Freshly baked Arab bread is stacked high and used to scoop up the selection of food. Eggs in a variety of forms are also favorites.

11

HOMESTYLE MIDDLE EASTERN COOKING

The main meal of the day can be in the middle of the day, but is usually served in the evening when the family is together. It consists of perhaps three dishes, which probably include meat, poultry, or fish, and one or two vegetable dishes. A grain dish that is often rice and bread are the staples and there will undoubtedly be relishes, yogurt, and a salad. The main course is followed by fruit and nuts, sweets, pastries, and coffee.

The lighter meal of the day will often consist of a selection of mezzehs.

Between meals snacking is regarded as the norm and, of course, the strong, thick coffee or tea is always bubbling away.

At mealtimes the men of the family are fed first. They take the best of the food and what is left is then eaten by the women and children—often in another room, while the men smoke their hubble-bubble pipes. Meals are taken seated on cushions around a low table or on a carpet. Before eating, a large ornate tray with a matching bowl and jug often made from hand-beaten copper, silver or for the wealthiest, gold, is brought in. The bowl contains warm soapy water and the jug contains water. Both hands are washed, rinsed, and dried before eating can commence.

The meal itself is served in large communal bowls. The diner selects the items of his own choice with his right hand only, and eats with it, using, in most Islamic countries, the thumb and first two fingers up to the second knuckle. Only at the end of the meal is it polite to lick the fingers. Westernized Middle Easterners, of course, are happy to use cutlery, but it was a former Shah who said, "Eating with a knife and fork is like making love through an interpreter."

A guest in a Middle Eastern home must never be refused hospitality, no matter how inconvenient. The ubiquitous Arab coffee is offered first, followed by snacks (or mezzeh). The guest must refuse these offerings at the time they are offered. He will be asked again and even a third time. He must eventually accept "under pressure." Not to go through this ritual is considered a lack of manners.

ALCOHOL

Alcohol is strictly forbidden to Moslems. In most of the Gulf countries, even non-Moslems are subject to severe punishment—public floggings, in some instances—if discovered drinking even in the privacy of their own homes.

Some Moslem countries are far more tolerant about alcohol, particularly those with a burgeoning tourist trade, or those with Christian populations. Many wines and spirits produced in these countries are now available in the West. If you can get hold of a locally produced bottle, it will add great interest to your meal.

Morocco

The vineyards are postwar French plantings. *Vin Gris de Boulaoune* and *Gris de Guerrovane* are pale dry rosés, *Sidi Larbi* and *Dar bel Amri* are reds. *L'Oustalet* is a white blanc de blanc. *Mahia* is a liqueur made from dates and figs.

Tunisia

By contrast the Tunisian vineyards are very ancient, many originating from 400 B.C. and the days of Carthage. *Muscat de Keliba* and *Château Khanguet* are good whites, and *Magon* and *Sidi Saad* are good reds. *Boukha* is a fig liqueur, *Thibar* a sweet brandy, and *sirop* is an ultra-sweet pomegranate liqueur. On the island of Jerba, *la'hmi* is a sour, fermented date liqueur.

Algeria

The French influence has enabled Algeria to produce a series of fine rosés and reds from the Mascara, Medea, and Dahra regions and reds from Zaccar and Tessala.

Egypt

It was the Pharaohs who first developed the art of wine making here. Early this century new Egyptian vineyards were established near Alexandria at Abu Hummus. Two good whites are *Reine Cléopatre* and *Cru des Ptolemées. Omar Khayyam* is a smooth red with a slight flavor of dates. *Arak*, also called *Zibib*, is a spirit distilled from wine and flavored with anise.

The Levant

Vineyards were established in 1857, by Jesuits in the Bekaa valley at Ksara. Two good wines from there are *Château Kefraya* (rosé) and *Château Musar* (red). Arak is also produced. There are also small vineyards in Syria at Halab, Homs and near Damascus and in Jordan at Az-Zarqa and Ram.

Israel

Baron Edmond de Rothschild laid down extensive vineyards at Mount Carmel near Tel Aviv in 1880, at the time when his French Chateau Bordeaux had reached the peak of excellence. Today a range of reds includes *Vin Fou, Avat* and the sweet *Adon Atic*, and white wines include *Carmel Hock* and the drier *Château de la Montague*. Sparkling wines are produced and there are even *kosher* wines.

Turkey

Turkey is the biggest wine producer in the Moslem world. Indeed, its vineyard is the world's fifth largest, although many of the grapes are eaten as fruit. The celebrated Turkish wines are a light red *Trakya*, from Thrace, and a robust dark red *Buzbag* from Anatolia. There is also a white *Trakya. Tckirdag* is a medium white. Raki is the Turkish version of Arak, drunk in Turkey with *mezzeh. Mersin* is a liqueur made from oranges.

Armenia

Archaeological evidence shows that the Armenians invented wine making over 3,500 years ago. The tradition has been maintained to this day and the area produces some of the region's best wines. Exports occasionally reach the West and are worth trying for curiosity value alone. Armenia is also a major producer of sherry, brandy, and vodka. *Oghi* is similar to Turkish *Raki* and Lebanese *Arak*.

A MIDDLE EASTERN MENU

Constructing a Middle Eastern menu is great fun because the range of options is enormous. I have organized the subsequent chapters into groups so that you can create a meal of one, two, three, or even four courses by bringing together your choice of dishes from the relevant chapters. Or you can put together a selection of snacks or quickly make a light supper or even breakfast.

If you wish, you can put together representative dishes of one country or area. Alternatively, and I think quite legitimately, your meal will be even more interesting if you construct your menu using the dishes of many Middle Eastern countries. They are all compatible. Here are a few menu examples doing it either way. You can find these recipes by consulting the index.

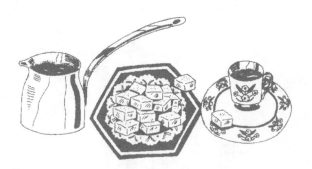

A Menu from Maghreb

Appetizer
Shorba bil hout (fish soup)

Main Course
Couscous served with Chicken Stew
(Chicken Tagine)
Spicy Potatoes (Batata Ma'li) served with
Chile Dip (Harissa)
Green Salad
Pickled Lemons (Limoon Makbous)

Dessert
Snake Cake (M'hancha)
Mint Tea (Chai Bi Na'Na)

A Menu from Israel

Appetizer
Avocado Dip with Puff Pastry
(Sabra Dip with Pastelle)

Main Course
Casserole of Beef/Lamb (Cholent)
Mixed Vegetables
Latkes Served with Bagels

Dessert
Cheese Blintzes (Blitzes)
Tea or Coffee with Stuffed Dates
(Sephardi)

A Menu from Egypt

Appetizers
Falafel
Mixed Salad with Bread (Fattoush)

Main Course
Quail Stuffed with Wheat
(Siman Bil Kibbeh)
Green Vegetables (Melokhia)
Broad Beans Served with Bread
(Ful Nabed served with Aiysh)
Mixed Salad
Garlic Dip (Taratoor B'sade)
Pickled Vegetables (M'qalel)

Dessert
Ali's Mom's Pudding (Um m'ali)
Arab Coffee (Q'ahwa Arabiya)

A Menu from the Levant

Appetizers (Mezzeh)
Sautéed Lamb Liver (Kibid Mili)
Tabouli
Grilled Lamb on Skewers Served with
Bread (Shashlik Kebabs served with
Khoubiz or Ka'ak)

Main Course
Stuffed Meat in Bulgur (Kibbeyets)
Stir-Fried Okra (Bamiya B'zayt)
Rice and Vermicelli (Roz bi Sha'riyah)
Pickled Vegetables (Torshi)

Dessert
Fried Semolina Pudding (Sujee Helva)

A Menu from Arabia

Starter
Crumbly Dip (Dukkah)
Green Bean Salad (Loubla B'zeyt)
Shrimps (Nachbous)

Main Course
Roast Lamb (Fakhid Kharouf)
Brown Lentils Served with Bread
(Ads bi Gibba served with Khoubiz)

Dessert
Sweet Crisp Shredded Pastries (Kadayif)
Arab Coffee (Q'ahwa Arabiya)

A Menu from Iran

Appetizers
Herbal Omelette (Kookoc, Sabzi)
Mint and Herb Salad
(Sabzi Isfahan Khodran)
Yogurt Drink (Abdug)

Main Course
Duck in Pomegranate (Faisinjan)
Chickpeas and Spinach
(Houmous ye Esfanaj)
Rice (Chellow)
Pickled Lemons (Limoon Makbous)

Dessert
Fresh Fruit
Tea with Sugared Nuts (Loze Hilou)

A Hot and Spicy Menu from Yemen and Oman

Appetizers
Heart, Kidney, and Liver Stir-Fry (Kirshuh)
Small Stuffed Pastry (Sambusak Boregi)
Yogurt Cheese in Oil (Labnah Makbous)

Main Course
Spicy Minced Meat
(Kiymeh Mashwi Omani) or
Spicy Roast Chicken (Djej Mechoui)
Stuffed Zucchini (Sheik-el-ma'shi)
Fenugreek Hot Dip (Hilbeh)
Rice with a Crispy Crust
(Chellow with Hakkakah) or
Spicy Bread (Saluf bi Hilbeh)
Vinegared Chiles (Qali Filfil)

Dessert
Syrupy Pancake (Ataif)
Yemeni Coffee (Q'shr)

A Menu from Turkey

Appetizer
Fried Mussels (Midye Izmiri Tavasi)

Main Course
Turkey and Chestnuts
(Kastelani Hindi Guveci)
Artichokes (Enginar)
Sautéed Celery (Tereyagli Kereviz)
White Rice (Beyaz Pilav)
Vinegared Chiles (Biber Tursu)

Dessert
Sweet Shredded Pastries (Kadayif)
Turkish Tea and Turkish Delight
(Chaiy Turki and Lokum)

A Menu of Middle Eastern Favorites
(Suitable for a party)

Appetizers (Mezzeh)
Chickpea Dip
(Houmous B'tahine)—Levant
Fish Roe Dip (Taramasalata)—Turkey
Stuffed Vine Leaves
(Dolmades)—Greece
Falafel—Israel
Pastries (Boreks and Breiks)—
Turkey/Maghreb

Main Course
Whole Spicy Roast Lamb
(M'choui)—Morocco
Lamb and Cherry Kofta
(Lahma-kafta bil karaz)—Saudi
Baked Curried Fish (Masgouf)—Iraq
Brown Beans (Ful Medamis)—Egypt
Ratatouille-Style Vegetables
(Chakchouka)—Maghreb
Rice (Pollou)—Iran
Turkish and Saudi Breads
(Pitta and Khoubiz)
Pickled Vegetables (Tursusu)

Dessert
Baklava, Kadayif and Fresh Fruit
Mint Tea, Coffee and Turkish Delight

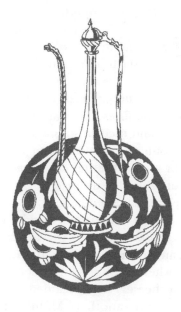

BASIC INGREDIENTS AND RECIPES

In this chapter I have collected information about basic flavoring ingredients. Middle Eastern cooking uses herbs quite extensively. Spices vary from country to country. The southern Gulf states such as Yemen and Oman use a lot of spices, especially hot ones. In northern Iraq and Tunisia, pungent spices such as chile and fenugreek are popular, while in Morocco, cumin, cinnamon, and pepper are widely used. Saffron, the prize of the Arabs, is used in many recipes, and garlic is universal. Nuts are important for both taste and texture, walnuts being the Caucasian favorite, hazelnuts in Turkey and Morocco, almonds and pistachios in Iran; pine nuts are the favorite in the Levant and the Gulf.

There are a number of spice mixtures used in different countries which are described in this chapter and used in subsequent recipes. In some countries most cooking is done in olive oil or clarified butter called *smen*. But a number of other oils are used to good effect, and these are examined here.

Yogurt plays a vital part in Middle Eastern cuisine. It is used as a dip as well as a sauce for cooking, and as a refreshing cold drink in hot countries where alcohol is forbidden. It is also made into cheese. I have included recipes for these and for another Middle Eastern favorite, pickles.

FRESH HERBS

Fresh herbs are used imaginatively in the Middle East. Some are familiar and easily obtained in the West, others are not exported and so are not available. Wandering around any *soukh* will reveal heaps and heaps of colorful fragrant herbs of so many varieties that it would be impractical to list them all if indeed that were possible, as some do not have English translations. The following list is therefore a mere whiff of the delights of the Arabian herb garden: basil, chervil, coriander, cress (*barbeen*), dill, fennel, garlic, chives, marjoram, *melokhia*, mint, parsley, purslane, rosemary, sage, and thyme.

For more information please refer to the Herbs section on page 171.

SPICES

No country uses more spices than the subcontinent of India. Next is the Middle East. This is not surprising considering the close historical links between Arabian Moslems, Persia, and India. Most spices are common to all three. Curry, however, is not used in Middle Eastern food, although some dishes are close to the taste of curry. In particular, the spicy Iranian meat or vegetable spicy stew *koresh* is not unlike curry (indeed, it is thought that the Iranian word *koresh* gave "curry" its name).

The most important cooking spices used in the various Middle Eastern countries are allspice, aniseed, barberry, bay leaves, caraway, cardamom (green), cassia, chile, clove, coriander, cumin, fenugreek, ginger, *mahlab*, nutmeg, paprika, pomegranate, poppy seed, saffron, sesame, *sumaq*, turmeric, and *za'atar*.

For more information about these spices please refer to the Spices section on page 173.

MIDDLE EASTERN SPICE MIXTURES

Unlike Indian dishes, which use several spices, whole and/or ground, Middle Eastern cooks frequently use just one or two to flavor their dishes. But in some countries combinations of spices are used. The following mixtures should be regarded as representative rather than definitive.

Aromatic Salt

This is salt, preferably sea salt, to which is added a light spice mixture. Ordinary salt can be used in its place, but the spicing adds a delicacy and subtlety to a recipe.

Bahar

A widely used ground mixture of three sweet spices, cinnamon, clove, and nutmeg. Sometimes a pinch of ginger and/or pepper is added. Allspice was brought to the Middle East from the Americas in the sixteenth century. Its flavor was so similar to the above mixture that it was given the name *bahar* and now virtually replaces it.

Baharat

An Arab mixture of ground spices, normally including a combination of cinnamon, clove, coriander, cumin, nutmeg, paprika (for color), and pepper.

Chermoula or Tchermila

A marinating paste made by blending to a purée the following ingredients: 1 onion, 2 to 4 cloves garlic, 1 cup parsley or coriander, 2 to 4 red chiles or 1 to 2 teaspoons cayenne, 4 teaspoons paprika, 1 teaspoon salt, 1 teaspoon ground pepper, and 1 teaspoon saffron.

La Kama

From Tangiers in Morocco, this mixture includes ground spices in the following proportions: 2 parts black pepper to 2 ginger, 1 turmeric, 1 cinnamon and 1/4 nutmeg. It is used to flavor soups and stews.

Lebanese Mixture

This is a simple mixture of ground spices which can be used in soups or stews, or as a condiment sprinkled on the finished dish: 2 parts cinnamon to 2 paprika and 1 chile.

Ras-El-Hanout

This most celebrated Moroccan spice mix contains a mixture of around twenty (sometimes twenty-five) whole spices, dried herbs and flowers; it literally means "shopkeepers' choice," and there are as many variants as there are Moroccan spice sellers. It is a familiar sight in the markets, where the spice vendor will sell it by the teaspoon, kilo, or sack. As each vendor has his own secret blend passed down by word of mouth through generations, there are many variations. The ingredients list is, as you would suspect, not at all easy to extract from the salesman—even if one does, it is not always easy to understand what he will tell you in Arabic. I met a very bizarre trader who sat cross-legged on his mat in the spice market in Tetuane. As far as I could tell from my interpreter friend, this was what his *ras-el-hanout* contained: the spices—peppercorns (black and white), chile, cumin, coriander, cassia, nutmeg, whole green cardamom, cloves, mace, fenugreek, and black cumin; the dried flower petals—rosebuds, orange blossoms, lemon blossoms, belladonna berries, saffron, German iris, lavender; and cantharides (Spanish fly); the roots—ginger, galingal (lesser), wall broomgrass (*tharra*), and rhizome of ash tree; the herbs—rosemary, thyme, *harmel*, *jusquiane*, grains of paradise, and java almond (*bsibsa*).

The end result is used to flavor such dishes as *tagine*, and its use is said to increase vigor, health, and longevity, not to mention virility.

Ta'leyah or Taqliya

A mix of onion fried with garlic used as a garnish, chutney ,or baked on bread (see page 40). A Yemeni variant, *talia*, includes chile.

Tahini

Tahini is regarded as a staple and is simple to make. Sesame seeds are lightly roasted, then ground and mixed with sesame or olive oil to make a smooth, stiff paste. Salt and garlic can be included optionally. *Tahini* is also available canned or bottled from commercial sources, but the quality differs widely.

Za'atar

This is the Arabic word for thyme, but can also mean a blend of powdered herbs and spices, which usually includes thyme, marjoram, *sumak*, and roasted sesame seeds.

Zhug

From Yemen, where they like hot food, this is a mixture of ground cumin, cardamom, and garlic, which are first fried to release the flavors. Then chiles and herbs such as fresh coriander are blanched and then combined and ground to a paste. Used as a fresh chutney within a day or two. With vinegar added, it will keep for up to a week in the refrigerator.

DRIED FRUIT

Dried fruit such as dates, figs, apricots, and plums are particularly popular in stews.

OLIVES

The olive is one of the earliest known "fruits." Originally a native of the Mediterranean, there are many varieties, differing in size, quality, color, and taste. The difference between white, green, purple, and black olives is simply the degree of ripeness. Eaten raw, they are too bitter to be palatable. Treated by prolonged immersion in brine or vinegar, they became familiar. In all the countries of the Middle East they are consumed with great satisfaction—plain, stuffed, or in cooking.

NUTS

Five indigenous nuts figure prominently in the Middle East: Almonds are used in Iranian and Turkish dishes; the Iraqis use hazelnuts, and walnuts are featured in Armenian and Georgian food. These nuts are used whole or crushed in both savory and sweet dishes and in salads. Roasted pine nuts (*snorbeh*) give a distinctive nutty taste when added to the cooking pot, and are especially popular in Egypt, Syria, and Lebanon. The creamy and succulent pistachio nut is a favorite garnish for sweet and savory dishes. It is frequently sprinkled on Iranian rice.

OILS AND FATS

There are a number of different oils and fats used in the Middle East.

Olive Oil

Used extensively for cooking and in salads, especially in Greece, Turkey, and the Levant. It has a powerful taste when used in cooking.

Sesame Oil

Used since ancient times, it is still a favorite with the Egyptian Copts and many others. It has a very distinctive taste, and prolonged cooking sweetens it.

Smen or Samneh

This is clarified butter. When allowed to cool it sets to a dripping-like consistency. Its color ranges from pure white to deep yellow and it has a delicious aroma which is imparted to food, especially subtle dishes such as rice. It is usually made from goat's or sheep's butter, and occasionally camel's butter. If made from cow's butter it is indistinguishable from Indian *ghee*. It was almost certainly an invention of the cattle-breeding Aryans, who took it to India and the Middle East. When cooled and set, it will keep for several months. *Smen* can also be made from margarine.

It is easy to make. Simply bring a couple of sticks of ordinary butter to a boil, then lower the heat, and simmer for half-an-hour or so. Strain it into a container, discarding the sediment. Apart from the wonderful flavor, its great advantage is that, having no impurities, it can be heated to a higher temperature than other oils, and food cooked in it is less likely to burn. Vegetable ghee is a less expensive substitute with similar properties to samneh, but it has less flavor. All are highly saturated.

Other Oils

Any oil is suitable for cooking. Vegetable or corn oils are inexpensive and neutrally flavored. For the health-conscious, light mono- or polyunsaturated oils such as sunflower or soybean oil may be used. Samneh and ghee congeal when exposed to air and so are unsuitable for salads or cold dishes. Hazelnut and walnut oils are, in my view, two of the most delightful aromatic oils available and are perfect for salads; however, they are quite expensive and their subtlety is lost in cooking.

GARLIC (*THAWM OR TUM*)

Garlic probably originated in Turkestan and Siberia. The ancient Egyptians valued it highly, believing that a bulb of garlic represented the cosmos, with each clove a part of the solar system. It was fundamental to their diet, and 15 pounds of garlic would buy one slave. Indeed, an inscription on the Great Pyramid of Cheops states that the slave builders were supplied with garlic and radishes daily for health reasons. History's first recorded industrial dispute took place 3,000 years before Christ, when these slaves mustered up the courage to go on strike because their garlic ration was cut. Garlic was found in Tutankhamun's tomb, probably to ward off the evil eye.

The Babylonians of 3000 B.C. considered garlic to be a medicinal miracle, as did the ancient Greeks. In 460 B.C. Hippocrates extolled its virtues, as did Aristotle eighty years later. Aristophanes believed it enhanced virility. The Phoenicians carried garlic in their Mediterranean trading ships and the Talmudic Kosher rules of the Hebrews prescribe when and where garlic may be used. The Prophet Mohammed also respected garlic, recommending its use to counteract the stings and bites of venomous creatures such as scorpions. He delighted in eating raw onion and garlic, yet he warned that they could have powerful aphrodisiac qualities. He had a vision of Satan in the Garden of Eden with onion on the ground at his left foot and garlic at his right.

Garlic is indispensable in today's Middle Eastern cooking. It grows everywhere, and is used both raw and cooked, sometimes subtly, sometimes overpoweringly. It even appears in certain sweet dishes.

YOGURT

Yogurt predates written history. It is milk into which a culture of bacteria is introduced. Then the mixture is left to rest at a constant temperature to induce fermentation, souring, and coagulation. One theory on how yogurt came about is that the ancient tribes, probably the dairy-farming Aryans, carried their spare milk in leather pouches. Some bacteria may have got into the pouch and the heat of the desert sun did the rest.

Today it is a staple all over the area. It is known as *laban* in Arabia, Egypt, and the Levant, as *mast* in Iran, *mazdoon* in Armenia, and *jiaouru* in Greece. *Labnah* is the Arabian version of yogurt cheese, which is made simply by straining ordinary yogurt through muslin overnight and shaping the soft curds into balls. Taken at breakfast in Armenia, this is called *banir* and in Turkey *peynir*— both closely related to India's *paneer*.

AROMATIC SALT

Throughout this book, recipes will call for aromatic salt. Here are two recipes, the first being light and aromatic, the second containing spicier flavors and the richness of good nuts. Finely grind a good size batch and store in an airtight container.

LIGHTLY SPICED SALT

INGREDIENTS

1/2 cup coarsely granulated sea salt

1 teaspoon powdered cinnamon

1 teaspoon ground allspice

SPICIER AROMATIC SALT

INGREDIENTS

1/2 cup lightly spiced salt

1/2 teaspoon ground fenugreek seed

1 teaspoon dried mint

1 tablespoon very finely ground almonds

1/2 teaspoon turmeric

Home-Made Yogurt

MAKES ABOUT
15 OUNCES
YOGURT

Making yogurt is a skill well worth mastering. Not only does home-made yogurt cost a fraction of factory versions, but it is fresher and creamier too. To start a yogurt you need fresh milk. You also need a live bacteriological culture called *bulgaris*, to start the process. As bulgaris is present in yogurt you can use commercial yogurt as a starter, although this is weaker than proper culture and may result in a thinner yogurt. However, this can be thickened with powdered milk.

If you decide to make yogurt regularly, a good investment is a cooking thermometer or, better still, an electric yogurt-maker.
Successful yogurt-making depends on:
(**a**) boiling the milk, which ensures there are no competitive bacteria left alive to compete with the bulgaris in the yogurt,
(**b**) using fresh culture or yogurt as the starter,
(**c**) keeping the newly mixed yogurt warm enough to ferment and multiply for the first few hours, and
(**d**) stopping fermentation by chilling to prevent it from becoming sour.

INGREDIENTS

2 cups fresh, whole milk

1 tablespoon powdered milk (optional but gets thick results)

1 tablespoon bulgaris culture or fresh yogurt

METHOD

▪ In a 2-quart saucepan, bring the milk to a boil. Add the powdered milk, lower the heat, and simmer for 2 to 3 minutes.

▪ Remove from the heat and allow to cool for about 30 minutes to just above human body temperature (to between 104°F and 113°F). If you don't have a food thermometer, test as you would a baby's formula by placing a few drops on your wrist.

▪ In a mixing bowl, combine the yogurt culture or commercial yogurt with a few drops of the warmed milk. Mix well. Continue to add milk a little at a time until it reaches pouring consistency.

▪ Pour this mixture and the remaining milk into a nonmetal bowl. Cover the bowl with plastic wrap and place in a warm, draft-free place to ferment (a prewarmed oven with heat turned off works well).

▪ Allow to ferment undisturbed for at least 6 hours but no more than 8. (The longer it is left the more sour it becomes.) Refrigerate (to stop fermentation) for at least 2 hours before serving.

Note: Fermentation will stop if temperature exceeds 130°F or goes below 100°F.

Strained Yogurt (Cheese)

LABNAH

Another staple in the Arab culinary repertoire, strained yogurt resembles cottage or feta cheese. It is easy to make, it keeps well, and is a wonderful way to use up surplus yogurt. It is traditionally salted and stored in olive oil spiced with chile peppers and herbs.

INGREDIENTS

muslin or a clean tea towel	any quantity yogurt

METHOD

■ Line a sieve or strainer with the muslin or tea towel and place over a large bowl or basin in your kitchen sink.

■ Pour the yogurt into the center of it. Gather up the four corners of the cloth and tie them together. Hook them over the sink tap so that the yogurt drips into a basin. Leave for at least 10 hours.

■ Remove the block of cheese from the cloth and crumble and store in an airtight container in the refrigerator.

■ You can also roll the crumbled cheese into small, marble-sized balls and place them in screw-top jar(s). Fill to the top with olive oil in which a pinch of salt, a dash of cayenne (optional), and dried herbs such as tarragon have been premixed. Use the fresh labnah within 3 days. The oil version, called *labnah makbous*, should be used within 10 weeks.

Yogurt Drink

ABDUG OR AYRAN

SERVES 1, APPROXI-MATELY 1 CUP (8 OUNCES)

In this recipe, yogurt is watered down and salt or sugar is added. It is best served chilled or, better still, with crushed ice—a luxury not usually afforded to the peoples of those hot countries. It is refreshing and nutritious, especially popular in Iran, where it is called *abdug* or just *dug*. In Armenia it is *tahn*, and elsewhere it is called *ayran* or *ayraan* or *laban* (which also means yogurt or yogurt drink) or *lben* in the Maghreb.

The Iranian version is likely to include fragrant additions described as options below. It can also be made with spring or carbonated water.

INGREDIENTS

1/3 cup yogurt	11/3 teaspoon powdered cinnamon (optional)
1/3 cup water	
1/3 cup crushed ice	1/3 teaspoon dried mint (optional)
1/3 teaspoon aromatic salt (see page 23 or sugar	1/3 teaspoon rosewater (optional)

METHOD

- Combine all the ingredients except the ice and blend.

- Put the ice into a chilled tumbler and pour the yogurt mixture over it.

YAHNI

(STOCKS)

MAKES 4 CUPS **A** good stock is an essential ingredient in many Middle Eastern dishes. Where a recipe calls for stock, use this spicy liquid, easily made according to a classic Arab recipe. For an even richer flavor, use 8 ounces meat scraps and bones, adding them at the same time as the rest of the ingredients. Store in airtight containers in the freezer for future use.

Yahni

INGREDIENTS

10 cups water	10 whole green cardamom pods, ground
2 cups chopped onion	2 teaspoons ground baharat (see page 19
4 cloves garlic, chopped	6 bay leaves
1 tablespoon smen (see page 21)	2 teaspoons aromatic salt (see page 23)

METHOD ■ In a stockpot or large kettle, bring the water to a boil and add the rest of the ingredients.

■ Lower the heat and simmer, covered, for 1 hour by which time the stock will have reduced by half.

■ Strain the liquid through a fine sieve or strainer, discard the solids, and use as required or store as above.

Pickles

TORSHI

Pickles have been around for thousands of years in the Middle East. Sealed earthenware jars of *torshi* have been unearthed by archaeologists in sites as far apart as Turkey, Syria, Egypt, and the Maghreb. Originally, the fruit or vegetables were pickled to last only for a few months, for use during the non-growing period, and for that reason the items were often pickled unblanched. But if the pickle is to be kept for six months or more, the item should be blanched and the vinegar to water ratio should be reduced to equal parts or the water even omitted. This reduces the chance of the item going bad. Unfortunately, fruits or vegetables that have been blanched will not be as crisp.

Typical pickling vegetables are turnip, eggplant, carrots, celery, green beans, cucumber, cauliflower, mixed vegetables, and green tomato. Fruit pickles can include cherry and peach.

INGREDIENTS

2 cups suitable vegetable or fruit (see above)
10 cloves garlic, halved

PICKLING LIQUID

1 cup distilled vinegar
2 cups water
2 tablespoons salt

METHOD

■ Clean and prepare the vegetable or fruit, slice or chop into strips, quarters, or squares, as appropriate.

■ In a large stockpot, bring water to a boil in the amount of 8 quarts of water to each pound of vegetables. Place the vegetables in a wire basket or larger strainer and submerge in the boiling water and wait until the water again reaches a full boil. Then begin timing the blanching, 6 to 8 minutes for denser vegetables such as cucumbers or carrots, 4 to 5 minutes for less dense vegetables such as eggplant and cauliflower, and 1 to 2 minutes for soft fruits and leafy vegetables. Shake the basket occasionally during the boiling process to ensure even cooking. When finished lift the basket from the boiling water and immediately plunge it into a pan of ice water to stop cooking. Chill until the vegetables or fruits are completely cool.

■ Fill mason jars or other airtight containers with the cooled fruit or vegetables and divide the garlic cloves evenly among them.

METHOD
- In a bowl, mix the vinegar, water, and salt and then pour the mixture into the jars. Jiggle the jars around to burst any air-pockets. Then top up each jar and seal. Store in a cool, dark place.

- Keep any spare pickling liquid for future use, in its own jar.

- Check the pickles after 48 hours to see they are settling. Often more liquid needs to be added to keep the pickles completely covered.

- The pickles are best if allowed to cure for at least two weeks.

Vinegared Chiles

BIBER TURSU

I am including this recipe by special request. Chiles are popular with many Middle Eastern heat-lovers, and vinegared chiles are especially popular in Turkey, the Levant, Yemen, and North Africa. Factory-bottled vinegared chiles can be found in specialty stores and the best of these come, in my view, from Cyprus.
Use the small, thin green or red fresh chiles, whichever you prefer.

INGREDIENTS

2 cups hot green or red chiles	2 teaspoons sugar
1 cup distilled vinegar	1/2 teaspoon salt
1/2 cup white wine	

METHOD
- Rinse and dry the chiles but do not trim the stalks.

- Pack the chiles into mason jars or other airtight containers

- Mix the remaining ingredients together in a pitcher and fill each of the jars to the brim. Shake them to burst air-pockets and top up if necessary. Leave in a cool, dark place for three or four days. Check the chiles periodically and top up with spare liquid or vinegar if needed. Leave for at least four weeks before using.

Pickled Lemon

LIMOON MAKBOUS

All over the Middle East, pickled lemon is one of the highlights of a meal, its tartness contrasting so well with the rich tastes of the main dishes. *Limoon makbous* are also used to liven up cooking, particularly in Iran and North Africa, and there are a number of variations.

TRADITIONAL METHOD

INGREDIENTS

salt	sunflower oil
4 lemons or limes, sliced	

METHOD

■ Sprinkle two or three large dinner plates liberally with salt.

■ Place the lemon slices onto the plates, sprinkling the tops with more salt. Leave for about 24 hours, during which the salt extracts the bitterness from the fruit.

■ On the following day, transfer the slices into mason jars, carefully piling up layers. When each jar is nearly full add just enough oil to fill them to the rim.

■ Leave the slices to cure for at least a month before using.

ALTERNATIVE METHOD

INGREDIENTS

4 lemons or limes	pickling liquid (see page 28)
salt	

METHOD

■ Cut each of the lemons or limes into six or eight wedges. Spread them on salted plates, sprinkle with more salt, and leave for at least 24 hours.

■ On the following day, transfer the wedges into mason jars, packing them tightly. Add enough pickling liquid to fill each of the jars to the brim.

■ Store in a cool, dark place for three to four weeks before using.

APPETIZERS, SNACKS, AND FINGER FOODS (MEZZEH)

▲▲▲▲▲▲▲▲▲▲▲▲▲▲▲▲▲▲▲

The mezzeh table is a uniquely Middle Eastern phenomenon. Mezzeh are small tidbits of food, each on its own serving plate, from which diners make their own selection. They are served as snacks, or as appetizers with various beverages, cocktails with coffee, or even as complete meals in themselves.

A guest in a Middle Eastern household, whether expected or not, must, as a matter of courtesy, be offered at least a small mezzeh selection, even if it is no more than olives, cheese, or dates.

There must be a number of dishes to make mezzeh and the more the better: invention and ingenuity are the keys to success. Most of us in the West have encountered mezzeh at our local Greek, Turkish, or Lebanese restaurant, where they are served as appetizers. They are always very pleasant (and often very filling), but the range is usually limited to a few trusted favorites of perhaps half a dozen choices. In the Middle East, it is a matter of pride as to how many are prepared. Mezzeh do not appear with every meal, but when they do, the average home cook may prepare eight or ten choices, and when entertaining, perhaps up to twenty. Restaurants average forty to fifty. A prestigious establishment or a caterer for a celebration party such as a wedding or a birthday will prepare up to as much as four times more!

The word mezzeh is probably derived from the Greek word *maza*, meaning mixture. In Tunisia mezzeh are called *aadou*, and in Algeria they are known as *kemia*.

Some mezzeh are simple to prepare—nuts, olives, cheeses, raw vegetables, and fruit, for example. Salads can be simple or complex, and a variety of cold puréed dips inevitably appear, the best known are hummus and taramasalata. Hot soups from thick stews to light broths are also popular. Stir-fried and deep-fried items give the mezzeh selection zest and interest, and are brought to the table sizzling hot.

The recipes in this chapter are a cross-section of mezzeh items, but you can also add items from the other chapters in this book. Always serve one or more types of Middle Eastern bread as accompaniment.

Chickpea and Sesame Dip

HUMMUS B'TAHINI

SERVES 4

Probably the best-known Middle Eastern dish, this is a purée made from chickpeas (hummus) and sesame seed paste (tahini). The texture of this dip ranges from quite coarse and porridge-like to very smooth. The texture is determined by the amount of grinding. Traditionally, it is hand-ground with a mortar and pestle, while a food processor does the job in seconds. A blender will require added water, so this will result in a runnier texture. This recipe freezes well and I like to make a large batch (three times this recipe) to have on hand for drop-in guests. Adjust the quantities of the garlic, lemon, and oil to suit your palate. Olive oil is traditional, but its powerful flavor is not to everyone's taste. Try hazelnut oil for a delicious variation.

INGREDIENTS

1 cup chickpeas	1 to 3 tablespoons lemon juice
3 tablespoons tahini (see page 20)	1 to 3 tablespoons olive or hazelnut oil
1 to 4 cloves garlic	salt to taste

METHOD

■ Pick through the chickpeas, removing discolored ones and any debris. Rinse the chickpeas and place them in a 2-quart saucepan or bowl with 4 cups of cold water. Let them soak for at least 12 hours, during which time they will swell in size.

■ In a separate saucepan, bring 4 cups of water to a boil. Rinse and strain the chickpeas and place them in the boiling water to simmer for about 45 minutes.

■ When they are soft, strain and run under cold water or set aside to cool. You can freeze the whole, cooked chickpeas at this stage for future use.

■ If using a food processor, simply place the chickpeas with the other ingredients, and blend until smooth. The longer the mixture is processed the finer the texture will be. Add a little water to assist the processor as needed. If using a blender, you will need more water. Grinding by hand is slow. Start with the peas first, adding the remaining ingredients as you achieve your purée.

■ Chill in the refrigerator for at least 30 minutes before serving with hot Arab bread and a salad.

Quick Hummus B'tahini

SERVES 4

INGREDIENTS

1 14-ounce can cooked chickpeas	1 tablespoon lemon juice
3 tablespoons tahini paste (see page 20)	2 tablespoons olive or hazelnut oil
1/2 to 2 teaspoons garlic powder	salt to taste

METHOD

- Strain the contents of the can setting aside the liquid. Grind the chickpeas to the texture of your choice, using as much of the liquid from the can as you need.

- Mix with the remaining ingredients. Serve chilled.

Salted Fish Roe Dip

TARAMASALATA

SERVES 4

Equally well known in the West is this creamy, pink-colored dip. Originating in ancient Greece, it is also found in Turkey, the Caucasian countries, and with slight variations throughout the Levant and the Gulf. The key to both taste and color is the fish roe from mullet (*tarama*). This lobster-colored roe is available salted and dried or bottled or canned. If you can obtain *tarama* from a specialty market you will be sure of the authentic taste, but a close substitute is smoked cod's roe. The bright rose pink taramasalata of the Western delicatessen is often "enhanced" with red food coloring. Yesterday's pita bread is always used in taramasalata to "soften" the flavor and to bulk out the purée. You can substitute regular bread, white or wheat, the latter giving a better taste and color than white, in my view. This dish can be made in larger quantities (triple the recipe) and frozen.

INGREDIENTS

1 pita bread or 2 slices white or wheat bread, crusts removed	1 to 3 tablespoons olive oil
	1 teaspoon red food coloring (optional)
1/2 cup salted tarama or smoked cod's roe	parsley, fennel, or cilantro sprig
1 to 4 cloves garlic, chopped	dash paprika
1 to 3 tablespoons lemon juice	1 black olive

METHOD

■ In a food processor or blender, grind the pita or bread into soft "crumbs."

■ Add the remaining ingredients and pulse them in the machine until they are mixed together. Add a little water to achieve the puréed texture of your choice.

■ Garnish with a sprig of parsley, fennel, or cilantro, a dash of paprika, and a black olive. Serve chilled with hot pita bread and a salad.

Quick Taramasalata

SERVES 4

INGREDIENTS

1/2 cup roe or smoked salmon	1 to 3 tablespoons olive oil
1/2 cup thick yogurt or cream cheese	dash paprika
1/2 to 2 teaspoons garlic powder	sprig parsley
1 to 3 tablespoons lemon juice	

METHOD

■ Combine all of the ingredients in a food processor and pulse until the desired texture is achieved. Garnish with a dash of paprika and a sprig of parsley and serve chilled with warm pita bread or raw or pickled vegetables.

Avocado Dip

SABRA DIP

SERVES 4

Sabra is the term for those people born in the new Israel. It is also the name of a desert cactus. Avocados are relatively new to Israel, having been first planted in Palestine by Jewish settlers early in this century. They are now a major Israeli export.

Dips are as old as the Middle East itself, forming an important part of the mezzeh table. This fine new Israeli recipe is ideal as an appetizer when served with "dip sticks" such as celery, cucumber, carrot strips, raw mushrooms, potato crisps, etc., and, of course, with hot pita bread. It can also be served as an accompaniment to the main course.

INGREDIENTS

1 ripe avocado	3/4 cup cottage or cream cheese, or sour cream, or strained yogurt, or a combination
1/2 green bell pepper	
1/2 cup chopped onion	milk
3 tablespoons lemon juice	salt to taste

METHOD

■ Cut the avocado in half, remove the pit, and scoop out the flesh into a food processor or blender. Add the bell pepper and onion and then add the remaining ingredients and combine thoroughly. If preparing it by hand, mash the avocado, finely chop the bell pepper and onion, then fold in the remaining ingredients.

■ Use the milk to obtain the desired texture and add salt to taste. Cover and chill in the refrigerator for at least an hour before serving. The lemon juice minimizes discoloration, but if the dip develops a dark skin on top, carefully scrape this off before serving.

Hot Fenugreek Dip

HILBEH OR HULBA

SEVERAL
SERVINGS

This dip originated in the deep south of the Arabian Gulf. There are many variations such as the Yemeni version, for instance, which is a very hot chile paste that is spread on *khoubiz* (bread) before it is baked. With or without chiles, this dip is very spicy and rather an acquired taste, for fenugreek is bitter. I have considerably reduced the fenugreek level in this recipe, but even so, it is not for the faint-hearted. Soaking the seeds until they soften and swell, with a jelly-like coating, removes some of the bitterness. Use as a dip or as an accompaniment to a main dish.

INGREDIENTS

2 tablespoons fenugreek seeds	1/4 cup chopped cilantro
4 tablespoons olive oil	3 to 4 canned plum tomatoes
4 to 8 cloves garlic, chopped	3 tablespoons lemon juice
1/2 cup chopped onion	2 to 6 fresh green chiles, stemmed and chopped
1 teaspoon ground baharat (see page 19)	

METHOD

■ Pick through the fenugreek seeds, removing any debris. Place them in a bowl with 1/2 cup cold water, and let soak for at least 12 hours or overnight.

■ In a medium skillet or wok, heat the oil and fry the garlic for 1 minute. Add the onion and sauté that for 3 minutes, stirring frequently. Strain the fenugreek seeds and add them to the skillet, stirring for 3 more minutes. Add the baharat and cilantro. Continue to sauté for another 3 minutes and then let cool.

■ Place the remaining ingredients into a food processor or blender and pulse into a purée.

■ Add the cooled sautéed mixture and continue pulsing to a thick purée.

Hot Red Chile Purée

HARISSA

Harissa is a spiced chile sauce which accompanies dishes of the North African countries. This particular recipe comes from Tunisia, where they like their food particularly hot. (The Algerian version is called *dersa*, and the Moroccan *felfel sudani*.) The texture should be fine but thick, and the color deep red, rather like tomato sauce or ketchup. Fresh red chiles should be used for the color, and in order to achieve the fine texture, the chiles and tomatoes should be seeded. This sauce is really meant to be extremely hot, and those who adore heat should add the cayenne and omit the red bell peppers.

Harissa is available canned in specialty stores, but it is easy to make at home. It will keep in the refrigerator for several days, and it freezes well. Make a large batch—double or triple the amount below—then freeze it for future use.

INGREDIENTS

20 fresh red chiles or 5 fresh red chiles and 2 red bell peppers	1 teaspoon ground cumin
4 canned plum tomatoes	1 teaspoon ground coriander
2 cloves garlic, chopped	1 to 4 teaspoons cayenne (optional)
	vinegar

METHOD

■ Stem and seed the chiles, the red bell peppers, and the tomatoes.

■ Place all the ingredients, except the vinegar, in a food processor or blender and process for 3 minutes to achieve a very fine texture. Add just enough vinegar during processing to ensure it turns into a stiff paste.

■ If you are preparing this the old-fashioned way, use a pestle and mortar and grind it all to a purée.

Garlic Dip

TARATOOR B'SADE

SEVERAL SERVINGS

Middle Easterners adore garlic, as an encounter with any friendly Arab will prove. They say if you can't beat 'em join 'em but beware—this dish is totally uncompromising: It is pure, raw garlic. So if you have someone to impress or flatter over the next day or two, do not eat this dip!

I like to make a large batch and freeze it in small containers. To avoid tainting everything else in the freezer, I remove the frozen dips from their containers and wrap each block in a plastic bag and seal it. I then put all the bags in one large bag and seal it and store it in a plastic lidded box.

INGREDIENTS

30 to 40 cloves garlic, chopped	3 tablespoons lemon juice
6 tablespoons olive oil	salt to taste

METHOD

■ Place all the ingredients in a food processor or blender and purée to the desired texture using water as needed.

Crumbly Spicy Nut Dip

DUKKAH

SEVERAL
SERVINGS

Dukkah is the name given to any dry mixture of spices, herbs, and nuts. Also called *do'ah* and *za'tar*, these mixtures are sold by street traders in twists of newspaper to eat there and then as an appetizer or to add as a condiment to a main dish. Variations of this dip are found all over the Middle East.

This dukkah recipe is from Egypt, and it is eaten with aish (Egyptian bread), which is first dunked in olive oil and then into the dukkah bowl. The dish has been enjoyed in Egypt since the time of the pharaohs, and was consumed by slaves and rulers alike. Dukkah was undoubtedly supplied in the pyramids to sustain their occupants on the long journey to the hereafter, and has survived into contemporary times as a poor man's meal. Today it is likely to appear as one of many dishes on the mezzeh table.

The important thing to remember about dukkah is that it should be dry and crumbly. It is easy to over-grind the ingredients, especially the nuts, which makes the mixture hot and oily. To prevent this, cool the ingredients after roasting, then proceed *slowly*.

INGREDIENTS

1/2 cup hazelnuts, shelled	1/2 teaspoon aromatic salt (see page 23)
1/4 cup sesame seeds	1 teaspoon za'atar (see page 20)
1 teaspoon coriander seeds	12 to 15 fresh mint leaves, chopped
2 teaspoons cumin seeds	

METHOD

■ Preheat oven to 325°F. Spread the nuts and seeds onto a baking sheet and bake for exactly 10 minutes. Remove and let cool completely.

■ When the nuts and seeds are cold, place them in a food processor (a blender doesn't work as well) with the other ingredients and pulse until the mixture is crumbly. Pause between pulses to prevent the mixture from overheating and becoming oily.

■ Serve as an appetizer or use as a condiment sprinkled over other dishes. The mixture will keep in an airtight container for several weeks, but if it does become stale after that time, you can add it to a Middle Eastern vegetable or meat dish to use it up.

Fried Garlic and Onion Garnish

TA'LEYAH OR TAQLIYA

SERVES 4

Originating in ancient Egypt, this simple garnish is used to liven up vegetable dishes which might otherwise be rather bland or as a garnish for any dish of your choice.

INGREDIENTS

4 cloves garlic	4 tablespoons olive oil
1 cup sliced onion	

METHOD

- Slice the garlic cloves into long thin strips, and do the same with the onion, crosscutting the strips so that they are approximately the same size as the garlic.

- In a skillet or wok, heat the oil to smoking.

- Add the garlic and onion to the oil and briskly sauté for 1 minute, then continue to sauté for another 5 minutes. The mixture should be well browned and crispy. Serve hot as a garnish.

Eggplant and Tahini Dip

BABA GANOUSH

SERVES 4

The eggplant is greatly relished all over the Middle East, and because it is very soft in texture, it works really well as a purée. This dish is particularly popular in the Levant, where it is called *baba ganoush,* and is often found in Lebanese restaurants in the West. Variations can also be found in Turkey, the Gulf, and Iran (where ground, dried fruit and yogurt are added to the purée). The dish should have an intriguing smoky taste, and this is obtained by baking the eggplant over charcoal until the skin is quite burnt. Then the pulp is scraped out and the skin discarded. Try this the next time you barbecue. The alternative is to grill it over low heat until it burns (turning it two or three times).

INGREDIENTS

2 1/2 pounds eggplant	2 or 3 pieces dried apricot (optional)
1 to 4 cloves garlic, chopped	1 tablespoon lemon juice
2 tablespoons tahini (see page 20)	salt to taste
2 to 4 tablespoons yogurt (optional)	pinch cayenne (optional)
	parsley sprig, chopped

METHOD

■ Wash the eggplant (do not trim the stalk). Prick it a few times with a fork or the tip of a knife.

■ Bake the eggplant over charcoal, or a low- to medium-heat broiler with the rack at lowest level, or in an oven preheated to 325°F. Cook until the skin has charred and blistered. Times will vary, but it will definitely cook for 20 minutes or longer. Check the eggplant and turn occasionally.

■ Remove from the heat, cut in half while still hot, and scoop out all the flesh, discarding the skin.

■ Place the cooked eggplant, garlic, tahini, yogurt, and apricot, if desired, into a food processor or blender, and pulse to a soft texture (or mash by hand). Add the lemon juice and salt to taste.

■ Serve cold, garnished with the cayenne, if desired, and parsley.

Cracked Wheat (Bulgur) Salad

TABOULI

SERVES 4

Tabouli is a very ancient dish that originally consisted largely of bulgur accompanied by mixed herbs, to create a substantial "peasant" meal. Modern recipes usually reverse the balance and the bulgur quantity is minimal. This recipe uses about 25 percent bulgur and the remaining ingredients are the salad vegetables of your choice. The quantity of bulgur can be increased or decreased to taste.

Provided that you are using bulgur (which is precooked, cracked, and dried wheat), no further cooking is required. Ordinary cracked wheat will require brief boiling. There are two ways of using bulgur for this dish, which is described below. Tabouli is a must as a mezzeh, or side dish. One attractive serving variation is to put the tabouli into "cups" of lettuce or vine leaves.

INGREDIENTS

1/2 cup bulgur	20 to 30 fresh mint leaves
1 head iceberg lettuce	4 tablespoons olive oil
10 to 15 cherry tomatoes	3 tablespoons fresh lemon juice
1 bunch scallions	1/2 teaspoon freshly ground black pepper
1 to 2 bunches parsley	1/2 teaspoon baharat (see page 19)
1/2 bunch cilantro	aromatic salt to taste (see page 23)

METHOD

■ If you prefer bulgur with a soft texture, soak it in 2 cups cold water for 20 minutes. Strain through a fine sieve to squeeze out all the excess water and set aside. If you prefer the bulgur to be crunchy, add it dry to the vegetable mixture.

■ Wash and chop the vegetables and herbs, then toss together in a large bowl.

■ Whisk the oil and lemon juice together and toss into the salad.

■ Add the bulgur, pepper, baharat, and salt. Toss once more and set aside (preferably in the refrigerator) for half an hour or so to allow the flavors to blend.

Toasted Bread Salad

FATTOUSH

SERVES 4

Arab bread, khoubiz, or pita, is delicious when it's hot and fresh, but left until next day it becomes hard and unappetizing. This ancient salad recipe provides a resourceful way of using up old bread. *Fattoush* literally means "wet bread" and traditionally the khoubiz was soaked in water, and slit along the edge into two discs, then it was toasted so that it became crisp. This recipe omits the soaking and you can use fresh or frozen and thawed Arab bread.

The salad vegetables here are suggestions—use any of your choice, but I do recommend the spinach, which is unusual. It can be substituted for *melokhia* (Egyptian) or *rijlah* (Arab) leaves; these are virtually unobtainable in the West and are mandatory in a real fattoush.

INGREDIENTS

2 pieces khoubiz or pita bread	10 to 15 fresh mint leaves
1 head iceberg lettuce	2 cloves garlic, minced (optional)
4 to 6 large spinach leaves	4 tablespoons olive oil
1 4-inch piece cucumber	3 tablespoons fresh lemon juice
1/2 cup chopped onion	1/2 teaspoon freshly ground black pepper
1 bunch fresh parsley	aromatic salt to taste (see page 23)

METHOD

- Slit open the bread along its edge to make two discs, then broil over low heat until crisp and golden. Or bake the bread in a preheated 325°F oven for 10 to 15 minutes. Remove from the oven, let cool, then cut into pieces about 1/2 inch square.

- Wash and chop the salad vegetables and herbs, and toss together in a large bowl.

- Whisk together the oil and lemon juice and toss into the salad. Set aside (preferably in the refrigerator) for about half an hour.

- Just before serving, toss in the pepper, aromatic salt, and the bread pieces.

Green Bean Salad in Olive Oil

LOUB'YEH B'ZAYT

SERVES 4

You won't travel far in the Middle East without encountering this delicious salad. Sometimes tomatoes are included, sometimes not, so I have made them optional. The beans normally used are thin string or runner beans, but Kenyan beans are perfect. This dish can be served hot, lukewarm, or even cold with hot khoubiz bread.

INGREDIENTS

3/4 cup string beans	1 teaspoon cayenne (optional)
4 tablespoons olive oil	1/2 teaspoon freshly ground black pepper
2 to 4 cloves garlic, chopped (optional)	aromatic salt to taste (see page 23)
1/2 cup chopped onion	1 tablespoon chopped cilantro
4 to 6 canned plum tomatoes, chopped (optional)	

METHOD

■ Wash and stem the beans, stringing them if necessary. Cut into 2-inch pieces.

■ Place the beans into 4 cups boiling water, lower the heat, and simmer for 5 minutes. Strain and set aside.

■ Meanwhile, in a skillet or wok, heat the oil and sauté the garlic and onion, if desired, for 3 minutes. Add the tomatoes and cayenne, if desired, and continue to sauté for 1 minute, mashing the tomatoes.

■ Add the strained beans and simmer for 5 minutes. Stir in the pepper, salt, and cilantro.

Mixed Herb Salad

SABZI ISFAHAN KHODRAN

SERVES 4

A delightful tradition at the Iranian dining table is the traditional appearance of a large, ornamental dish containing a mixture of as many varieties of fresh herbs that the host can obtain, some familiar, many that we have never seen in the West, some bitter, some sweet, all fragrant and tasty. Huge hot pieces of floppy nane lavash (bread) and yogurt or samneh are also served, and the diner scoops up the herbs and a little yogurt or samneh in a piece of bread, to enjoy a healthy and enticing appetizer. The bowl stays on the table throughout the meal, enabling the diners to garnish other dishes to their liking. If you are lucky enough to have a herb garden you can really have fun with this.

My combination varies somewhat, depending on availability, but it usually contains all of the first seven ingredients and one or two of the last four. Note that there is no dressing or seasoning as these would overwhelm the subtle flavor of the herbs.

INGREDIENTS

1 head chicory	1 bunch watercress
1 head endive	30 fresh mint leaves
1 bunch parsley	1 bouquet mustard greens
1 bunch chives	dill, basil, fennel, and marjoram sprigs

METHOD

- Wash, shake dry, and stem herbs, discarding any discolored or bruised leaves.

- Chop to your liking and toss together in a large bowl.

- For best (crispiest) results, cover the bowl, and refrigerate for at least 2 hours (and a maximum of 4).

45

Fish Soup

SHORBA BIL HOUT

SERVES 4 AS A SOUP, 2 AS AN ENTRÉE

This is one of the few Libyan recipes in this book, although variations of it, mainly differing in the spice content, will be found as far apart as Morocco and the Gulf. Soups such as this one are bubbling and ready to serve the moment the sun sets to break the day-long fast during Ramadan.

In the Middle East, a soup is not usually served as a first course. It is more likely to appear as the main dish with a variety of relishes, and you can make this soup more substantial by using less water. My personal preference for the fish is for smoked haddock—I like its color and salty taste—but you can use any white fish. Serve piping hot.

INGREDIENTS

1 pound smoked haddock or other white fish

6 cups water

1 recipe chermoula (see page 19)

4 canned plum tomatoes, chopped

4 parsley sprigs

METHOD

- Skin, bone, and cut the fish up into chunky pieces, averaging 2 inches in length.

- In a stockpot or large kettle, bring the water to a boil. Lower the heat and add the fish, chermoula, and tomatoes. Simmer for 20 minutes. (The soup can be puréed in a food processor or blender at this stage, a preference in many Middle Eastern households.)

- Serve in soup bowls, garnished with fresh parsley sprigs.

- As an entrée, halve the water content and stir during the cooking.

Fried Squid

MANTIQ MEHAMMER

SERVES 4 AS AN APPETIZER

A few years ago I was working on a contract in Tunisia. The job involved the importation of some equipment to the small island of Jerba. This involved a cast, it seemed, of dozens of Tunisian officials—customs, police, agents, taxmen—and tons of paperwork. The only highlights amid days of tedium in dusty, downtown Houmt Souk, were frequent visits to a tiny marketplace café. It had no name and no menu. But they served the best Tunisian food. This simple squid dish was one of them.

INGREDIENTS

3/4 pound squid	2 fresh green chiles, stemmed, seeded, and minced
4 tablespoons olive oil	
4 to 6 cloves garlic, minced	1 teaspoon turmeric
1/4 cup minced onion	2 teaspoons dried mint

METHOD

■ Wash the squid thoroughly, removing any unwanted membranes. Then cut into rings.

■ In a skillet or wok, heat the oil and sauté the remaining ingredients for 2 or 3 minutes. Add the squid and sauté for another 15 minutes. To prevent sticking, you may need to add a little water from time to time.

■ Serve sizzling hot with a side salad, lemon wedges, harissa (chile sauce) and khoubiz bread.

Harira Mdiq

LAMB AND LENTIL SOUP

SERVES 4

Harira is a thick-textured Moroccan soup—a gruel really—of which there are literally unlimited variations. It was originally a Berber hill people's dish. It still is simple, but you can have this dish as a house specialty in five-star hotels (at enormous expense) or at market food stalls (for pennies). It is eaten at breakfast and last thing at night and at all times in between. It also figures largely during the month of Ramadan. I was fortunate enough to obtain this recipe from a Berber who spent his summers as a lifeguard at a holiday hotel in the town of Mdiq in Mediterranean Morocco. Each winter he would exchange his jeans and Walkman for his Rif mountain home town and his striped Berber robes. (*Mdiq*, by the way, is pronounced *Mideek* by Europeans and something guttural and inimitable by the locals, sounding like a cough and a spit.)

INGREDIENTS

3/4 cup red lentils	1 red bell pepper, chopped
1/4 pound lean lamb, cut into 1/2-inch cubes	2 fresh green chiles, chopped (optional)
1 cup chopped onion	2 tablespoons chopped cilantro
1 tablespoon la kama (see page 19)	25 to 30 saffron threads
6 tomatoes, peeled and chopped	salt to taste

METHOD

▪ Pick through the lentils to remove any debris. Rinse the lentils, then soak them in 4 cups cold water for 1 hour. Strain and set aside.

▪ In a stockpot or kettle, bring 4 cups of water to a boil. Add the lentils, lamb, and onion, lower the heat, and simmer for 30 minutes, stirring occasionally.

▪ Add the la kama, tomatoes, bell pepper, and chiles, if desired, and simmer for another 20 minutes.

▪ Add the cilantro and saffron, and season with salt. Simmer for 3 or 4 more minutes and serve piping hot.

Ground Chickpea Croquettes

FALAFEL AND TA'AMIAH

SERVES 4

Both Israel and Egypt claim falafel as their own national dish. Historically the honors probably go to Egypt, where it is called *ta'amiah*. The Egyptian version is made from ground white fava beans (*ful nabed*) and is oval in shape, whereas Israeli falafels are made from ground chickpeas and are spherical. There is some evidence that falafels existed in Pharaonic times when the Jews were the slaves of Egypt. That they have survived in both cultures for 3,000 years is remarkable.

Once you have tasted the real thing, store-bought, commercial mixes will be disappointing. Luckily they are easy to make at home although they take a bit of time, but they are well worth the effort (I make a large batch and freeze the extras). Serve hot with salad, khoubiz bread, and hummus b'tahini.

INGREDIENTS

2 1/4 cups chickpeas	1 tablespoon chopped cilantro
1 tablespoon fresh yeast (optional)	1 tablespoon tahini (see page 20)
2 to 4 cloves garlic, chopped	1 tablespoon lemon juice
1/2 cup chopped onion	1 teaspoon aromatic salt (see page 23)
1 teaspoon ground cumin	dry breadcrumbs
1 teaspoon ground coriander	vegetable oil for deep-frying

METHOD

■ Pick through the chickpeas to remove any debris. Rinse and place them into a 2-quart saucepan. Add 6 cups cold water and allow the chickpeas to soak for at least 12 hours or overnight.

■ Strain, rinse, and grind the chickpeas to an even, coarse texture in a blender or food processor.

■ The yeast will partly leaven the mixture, creating lighter falafels, but it can be omitted. Stir the yeast into 3 tablespoons of warm water, and when completely dissolved, add it and all the remaining falafel ingredients to the ground chickpeas. Grind into a thick paste, adding water as needed.

■ Knead the mixture like bread dough, and let it stand in a warm place for 30 minutes to allow the yeast to take effect and the flavors to blend. Then, knead the mixture.

■ To make falafels of equal size, divide the mixture into quarters, then subdivide each quarter into 6 (if you want a total of 24 falafels) or 4 (if you want 16 larger ones). Or you can use a melon baller to obtain falafels of equal size and shape.

METHOD

■ On a clean work surface sprinkle breadcrumbs and gently roll each falafel into a sphere. When they are all formed, let them stand again in a warm place for 15 to 20 minutes, during which time you can heat up the oil for deep-frying to 375°F.

■ Then one at a time, place 8 falafels into the hot oil and fry until golden brown. Usually 10 minutes is enough, but the timing depends on the size of the falafel so keep your eye on them after 5 or 6 minutes.

■ Remove from the oil and rest on paper towels in a warm place until you are ready to serve them all. They can be reheated in the oven if necessary and they will freeze for later use.

TA'AMIAH VARIATION

In place of the chickpeas, use the same weight of dry white (skinless) fava beans (*ful nabed*). The remaining ingredients and preparation are the same, but instead of spheres, make football-shaped discs; and instead of bread-crumbs, press the discs into sesame seeds before frying.

Spiced Lamb Sausages

MERGUEZ

MAKES 12
SAUSAGES

Mediterranean sausage is a combination of chopped or ground meat (often beef or lamb), which is encased with spices, and hung to dry in the sun.

The origin of the sausage seems to lie with ancient Mediterranean mariners whose meat supply had to be safely preserved and conveniently packaged. The Phoenicians, the great sea traders of the first millennium B.C., whose bases were dotted all around the Mediterranean, probably introduced the concept to Spain, Italy, Armenia, and Tunisia. In those countries today are found sausages with a common heritage: in Spain the *chorizo*, in Italy the mortadella and salami, in Armenia the *gologig*, and in Tunisia and the Maghreb, the merguez. They are eaten as appetizers or used to flavor cooking. These days it is quite normal to find all or some of these items in good delicatessens.

It isn't practical to produce them exactly at home without detailed curing and long sun-drying, but this recipe for merguez produces a cooked sausage which can subsequently be frozen for later use. The only special ingredient is the casing. You can use edible artificial casings also available from butchers. This recipe makes 12 merguez (making any less is hardly worth the effort) and you can freeze the extras.

INGREDIENTS

1 1/2 pounds lean mutton, lamb, or beef	6 tablespoons olive oil
6 to 8 cloves garlic, crushed	2 teaspoons sea salt
1 tablespoon finely ground ras-el-hanout (see page 19)	4 1/2 feet sausage casing

METHOD

■ If you don't have an electric or hand meat grinder, ask your butcher to coarsely grind your meat. Place ground meat in a large mixing bowl.

■ Add the rest of the ingredients and mix thoroughly by hand. Put the mixture into a piping bag with a large nozzle.

■ Wash your hands, then tie one end of the casing into a knot. Cut the casing to about 1 1/2 feet in length, and fit the open end securely over the piping nozzle. Squeeze the meat mixture into the casing, pushing it along to the knotted end, but do not overfill. When evenly distributed, and one-third of the mixture is used, disengage the sausage and tie off the open end.

■ Now create three 1-inch gaps in the casing to create 4 sausages that are 4 inches in length. Gently spin the casing at each gap and tie it with cotton thread (I find trying to knot the casing usually splits it open). Squeeze the meat back up to each knot.

■ Repeat steps 3 and 4 twice more, to make 12 sausages.

■ Merguez are traditionally boiled or grilled over charcoal. I prefer to oven roast them—they stay intact that way.

■ Preheat the oven to 275°F. Place the sausages on a couple of baking sheets, allowing them plenty of space, and roast for 20 minutes. Turn them and raise the temperature to 350°F and roast them a further 20 to 30 minutes. Check the sausages again halfway through the cooking process, turning as necessary to prevent sticking and uneven cooking.

■ Serve hot or cold or use to flavor other dishes such as couscous meat stew or chakchouka.

Sautéed Liver

KIBID MILI

SERVES 4

What could be simpler than strips of liver, coated with a mixture of flour and spices, and fried in oil? Every country mentioned in this book has one or more recipes for this dish, under a wealth of different titles. In Turkey, for example, there is *ciger tavasi*; in Qatar there is *kibda bi tum*, which uses plenty of garlic; in Egypt they have a variation using goose liver, *kibda ma'liya*. In Libya they roll the liver in partially crushed cumin seeds and call it *kabda camman*.

The liver can be from lamb, sheep, calf, goose, chicken, or (but not for Jews and Moslems) pig. The cut can vary from whole livers to delicate strips. Above all the spicing of this dish varies from mere salt and pepper in Armenia to explosively hot and spicy in Tunisia and Yemen. This Iraqi recipe is medium-spicy.

INGREDIENTS

3/4 pound liver	6 to 8 tablespoons sesame oil
1/2 cup all-purpose flour	4 lemon wedges
1 to 2 tablespoons baharat (see page 19)	parsley (or other herbs) sprigs

METHOD

- Wash and trim the liver, then cut into strips averaging 1/2 x 3 inches.

- Mix the flour and baharat and spread on a wide plate, near the stove.

- Heat the oil in a wok or large skillet.

- Coat the first few liver pieces in the flour mixture and drop them straight into the wok. Stir-fry, then coat the next few pieces, continuing in this way until half the pieces are cooking. (This keeps the oil temperature up and prevents the flour from becoming soggy.)

- Fry each piece for about 5 minutes, moving the strips around so that they all cook evenly. Remove and drain on paper towels.

- Repeat the cooking process with the remaining liver pieces.

- Serve sizzling with a lemon wedge and herb garnish.

Batter-Coated Mussels

MIDYE IZMIRI TAVASI

SERVES 4 AS AN APPETIZER

The city of Izmir is in western Turkey, nestled amidst the islands and river mouths of the Aegean Sea, a truly beautiful part of the world. It is an ancient city founded over 2,000 years ago. It was then called Smyrna and was an important trading city during ancient Greek, Byzantine, and Ottoman times. Nowhere in the world is there better seafood than in this part of the Aegean, and this recipe, said to date back to those times, is from the excellent Buyuk Efes Oteli, Izmir's finest hotel.

You'll find this dish all over Turkey using different varieties of mussels. I have used the large orange-pink ones with dark, blue-black shells. To control your portions, ask the fishmonger for the exact number you want (but always get a few extras in case some are already open and can be eaten).

INGREDIENTS

40 fresh mussels	1 teaspoon aromatic salt (see page 23)
1/2 cup all-purpose flour	milk
1/4 cup corn flour	lettuce leaves
1 egg	4 lemon wedges

METHOD

■ In a deep bowl, mix the flours, egg, salt, and enough milk to make a batter the consistency of ketchup. Allow to stand for 20 minutes to blend.

■ Meanwhile, prepare the mussels. Remember to choose only those which are tightly closed. Scrub them well and remove the beards. Place cleaned mussels in a shallow pan with a little water and heat for a few minutes until they open. Remove the mussels from the shells. Discard any that are still closed.

■ In a skillet or wok, heat the oil to 375°F.

■ Immerse each mussel into the batter and drop it into the hot oil. Put no more than ten at once into the skillet (this keeps the temperature consistently high and the result crisper). Fry for about 4 minutes, then remove. Drain on paper towels and keep warm. Repeat until all the mussels are cooked.

■ Serve on a bed of lettuce or radiccio with a lemon wedge.

53

PASTRY ITEMS

▲▲▲▲▲▲▲▲▲▲▲▲▲▲▲▲▲▲

If the peoples of the Middle East are united about anything it is their love of pastry. It appears at most meals and in many forms, perhaps the most celebrated of which is filo pastry, that amazingly thin pastry first developed in ancient Greece. It appears in pastry recipes of all sorts, the most popular of which is undoubtedly the Turkish-inspired borek. Almost every Middle Eastern country now has its range of borek-style finger pastries of various shapes and sizes with a wide range of fillings, and they are all delicious. Equally well known and ubiquitous are the two filo pastry sweetmeats, baklava and kadaif: The former is a sandwich of crunchy filo sheets interleaved with crushed nuts and dripping honey and syrup; the latter a shredded filo version. Other uses of filo include larger pastry dishes, among them bisteeya (a Moroccan specialty, pigeon pie) and spanokopita (spinach and cheese pie from Greece, the heartland of filo) with its derivatives tyropita (egg and cheese) and kotopita (chicken).

Although filo is the star ingredient in Middle Eastern pastry making, it by no means has a solo role. Ordinary puff or short pastries also have their places in such recipes as the pastele, a lidded round puff pastry pot from Israel. A rather surprising recipe which I could not fail to give you is the Arabian pizza, lahma-bi-ajeen. Originating in the Gulf, this is a flat disc of pastry on which is baked a delicious savory topping.

The dishes in this chapter are a representative selection of pastries from the Middle East, covering as wide a variety of styles as possible.

FILO AND WARKAH

All over the Middle East, from Morocco to Saudi Arabia, to Turkey and Greece, there is a tradition of making pastries with a dough which is literally as thin yet as strong as tracing paper. The methods of making this vary quite markedly. Best known to us in the West is the Greek filo pastry. This is the same pastry used to make strudels. The dough for filo pastry is straightforward enough, being a mixture of flour, water, and oil. A modest lump, the size of a tennis ball, is kneaded until it is very elastic, then it is rolled and stretched until it is thin and translucent (the name comes from the Greek for "leaf"). Commercially, it is rolled to a sheet about 4 feet square: this is slightly hardened then cut into sheets, usually 20 x 12 inches, and sealed in packs of 12 or 24. It takes professionals years to master the skills required to make filo, and it is very difficult to make at home, requiring a special long thin rolling pin, patience, and practice. Factory-made sheets are excellent, however, and can be obtained fresh or frozen from good delicatessens. Chinese spring roll pastry can also be used.

The Maghreb has developed its own method of making translucent thin pastry. The Moroccan *warkah* is made by dabbing a wettish lump of dough on a hot griddle pan to create a 3-inch disc. This operation is repeated with overlapping dabs, perhaps 40 or 50 times, until a disc some 18 inches in diameter is created. This is lifted off the pan and the operation starts again. A professional pastry maker can create a stack of discs deftly and quickly, and it looks so easy, but it isn't. In fact, I have never succeeded in re-creating it at home—either the small discs are too thick or too thin, they end up full of holes and they don't stick together, or the big disc falls apart, and so on. Although it is not quite the same as *warkah*, filo can be substituted.

Filo pastry can be baked, pan-fried, and deep-fried. Being very thin, it is very crispy and crackly when cooked. Some recipes require it to be boiled when the texture is soft.

SMALL STUFFED PASTRIES

BOREK

The royal chefs of the Ottomans vied with each other to produce the most memorable creations for their masters. He that achieved such a feat was showered with accolades, praise, and occasionally gold and jewels, so a great deal of creativity happened in the Ottoman kitchens and wonderful things transpired. One of them was a series of tiny pastries in myriad shapes and fillings. They were called boreks and soon became popular in all parts of the seventeenth-century Ottoman world. The pastry was always translucently thin and was based on filo or warkah. The names in each country varied slightly, producing a series of permutations on the original borek. Today the shapes are many, and the fillings equally varied.

Doughs and Pastries

Pastry

Pastry	Country	Dough
borek/ borekler/ boregler	Turkey	yufka
burekakia	Greece	filo/phyllo/fila
boreg	Armenia	phyllo
boreka	Israel	
burak/sambusak	The Gulf	ajeen
	The Levant	
samboosek	Egypt	gullash
briek/brik	Tunisia	madsouka
bourek	Algeria	dioul
briouat	Morocco	warka/ouarka
	Iran	qotab/koteh

The Shapes

triangle
square or parcel or pillow
cylinder
cigar or cigarette (cigara)

spiral or coil (burma borek)

scimitar or half-moon
sphere or ball
semicircle

Traditional Combinations

Name	Filling	Shape
ispanakli boregi	spinach	triangle
bohca boregi	herbs & cream cheese	sphere
puf boregi	ground meat	shaped or layers
cigara boregi	cheese	cigarette or cigar
burma boregi	any	coil
sanbusak boregi	any	scimitar
su boregi	any	boiled layers

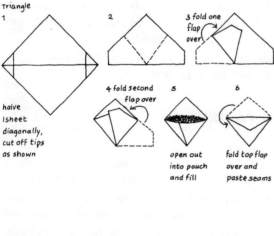

Triangle

1 halve 1 sheet diagonally, cut off tips as shown

2

3 fold one flap over

4 fold second flap over

5 open out into pouch and fill

6 fold top flap over and paste seams

Cylinder

1 square halved

put filling into area shown

fold over edges

roll up

paste seam

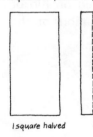

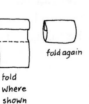

Square or parcel or pillow

1 square halved

filling

fold edges

fold where shown

fold again

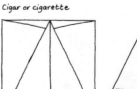
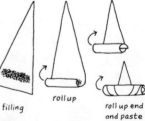

Cigar or cigarette

1 square cut as shown

filling

roll up

roll up end and paste

Dimensions

In the world of boreks, small is beautiful. Small also requires great skill to maintain this beauty. Boreks as small as 1 inch across are perfect mezzeh or finger foods, and look as good as they taste. Conversely, boreks can be as large as 6 inches across, when each one is virtually a meal in itself. The size of most boreks is somewhere in between.

The Fillings

Your imagination is the only limit when it comes to borek fillings. Traditional examples include ground or chopped meat, poultry, fish, or seafood, kibbeh, cheese, egg, and mashed or chopped vegetables such as potato or spinach, rice, lentils, and nuts. Suitable recipes in this book for borek fillings include the uncooked meat mixtures of ground chicken *(koftit ferakh)* (page 88), and ground meat with kibbeh *(kibbeyets)* (page 69), fish couscous *(kesksheh bil hout)* (page 102) drained and mashed, spiced shrimp *(nacbhous)* (page 100), and the filling of spanokopita (page 60), tyropita and kotopita (page 61).

Cooking

Best results are obtained by deep-frying or baking the boreks, but pan-frying and, in some cases, boiling are used. Deep-fry at 355°F for 35 minutes or until golden; bake in a preheated 375°F oven for 10 to 15 minutes or until golden; pan-fry in oil or *smen* for 5 to 10 minutes or until golden; boil in water for 5 to 10 minutes.

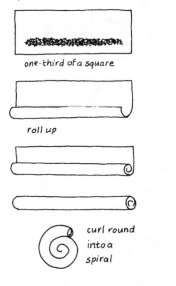

Spiral

one-third of a square

roll up

curl round into a spiral

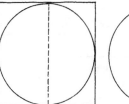

Semi-circle and scimitar or half-moon

one square or quarter square

cut into circle and fill

fold over, paste and press edges

shape into half-moon

Pigeon Pie

BISTEEYA

SERVES 4

Bisteeya, pronounced "pasteeya," loses considerably in its translation into English. It is indeed pigeon pie, but somehow calling it that does not in any way reveal what a delicious dish it is.

Many Moroccans regard it as their national masterpiece. Certainly it appears whenever there is something to celebrate. The real thing is difficult to make, requiring a couple of days, and the thinnest of warkah pastry: layers of it are built up and interleaved with alternate fillings of spicy pigeon and a sweet ground almond paste. This intriguing mixture of savory, sweet, and sour was probably introduced to the Maghreb from Persia over 1,000 years ago. Curiously, though, it is not found in the lands in between.

Bisteeya's traditional shape is round or octagonal, and after baking it is garnished with powdered sugar and ground cinnamon. I obtained this recipe from the excellent Bhaja Moroccan restaurant at Marrakesh's Hotel La Momunia. I have simplified it by using filo pastry, which is nearly as good.

INGREDIENTS

8 1/2-pound pigeons, oven-ready, or use equal weight of pheasant, partridge, or grouse	4 tablespoons brown sugar
	1 tablespoon powdered cinnamon
4 tablespoons lemon juice	2 to 3 tablespoons orange-blossom or rose water
1 recipe chermoula (see page 19)	
4 eggs, scrambled	clarified butter, melted
1/2 teaspoon aromatic salt (see page 23)	1 package commercial filo pastry (24 sheets of 12 x 20 inches)
1 tablespoon minced fresh mint	4 tablespoons Grand Marnier liqueur
1 tablespoon chopped cilantro	powdered or confectioner's sugar
1 cup ground almonds	powdered cinnamon or grated nutmeg

METHOD

■ Remove the skin from the pigeons and make small gashes in the flesh. Rub in the lemon juice and set aside for 2 hours.

■ Make the *chermoula* and cool.

■ Place the pigeons in a large non-aluminum casserole dish, rub them with the chermoula, cover, and refrigerate for at least 24 hours.

■ On the following day, preheat the oven to 375°F and bake the casserole for 30 minutes. Check occasionally during the cooking to ensure the casserole is dry but not dried up (add a little water if necessary).

58

METHOD

■ Remove and cool sufficiently to handle. (Keep the oven on.) Then remove the bones and unwanted matter. Chop the meat into small pieces. Mix in the scrambled egg, salt, mint, and cilantro.

■ To make the filling, in a separate bowl mix the almonds, sugar, cinnamon, and orange-blossom or rose water together so that they are crumbly and not too wet.

■ Select a round 9-inch baking pan and brush with melted smen.

■ Have a clean damp tea towel ready. Open the filo pastry packet and pull out all 24 sheets. Cut them together down to 12-inch squares with 12- x 8-inch rectangles.

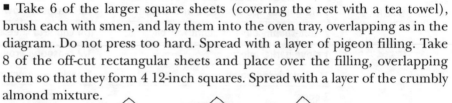

■ Take 6 of the larger square sheets (covering the rest with a tea towel), brush each with smen, and lay them into the oven tray, overlapping as in the diagram. Do not press too hard. Spread with a layer of pigeon filling. Take 8 of the off-cut rectangular sheets and place over the filling, overlapping them so that they form 4 12-inch squares. Spread with a layer of the crumbly almond mixture.

■ Repeat until all the sheets and all the fillings are used. Brush the top surface with melted smen, then fold the overhanging edges inwards to form an octagonal shape. Brush with Grand Marnier.

■ Bake for about 15 to 20 minutes until they are pale gold in color. Remove from the oven and carefully ease the pastry out of the baking pan. Invert and replace in the dish, brushing the top with Grand Marnier again. Bake for 10–15 more minutes. Remove when golden brown.

■ Again ease it out of the dish onto a serving plate. Turn it over and brush the top once more with Grand Marnier, then dust it with sugar and a grid of ground cinnamon as shown here for a really traditional look.

Spinach with Feta Cheese Pie

SPANOKOPITA

Although I had not intended to include Greek recipes in this book, spanokopita really cannot be omitted. It is a crispy filo pastry pie, traditionally filled with spinach, feta cheese, and herbs. It is normally made as a large pie which is cut into individual portions, but it can also be made into smaller triangles, discs, or coils. This recipe and its two sister recipes below come from Athens' wonderful Hilton Hotel restaurant, the Taverna ta Nissia. Follow the filo instructions for baklava on page 153 and remember to prepare the filling before opening the package of filo.

INGREDIENTS

1 1/2 pounds spinach, fresh or frozen	1/2 teaspoon powdered cinnamon
2 tablespoons olive or sunflower oil	1/4 cup feta cheese, crumbled
1 clove garlic, minced	1/2 teaspoon aromatic salt (see page 23)
1/2 cup minced onion	1 package commercial filo pastry
2 eggs	1/4 cup clarified butter
4 tablespoons each of minced parsley, cilantro, and mint	

METHOD

■ To make the filling, clean and chop the fresh spinach. In a stockpot or steamer, bring water to a boil and cook or steam the spinach for 15 minutes. If using frozen spinach, cook according to the package instructions. Drain, extracting as much water as possible, and set aside.

■ In a skillet or wok, heat the oil and sauté the garlic and onion until golden for about 10 minutes. Then add the spinach and continue to sauté over medium heat.

■ Beat the eggs in a bowl, and add the remaining ingredients. Pour this mixture into the frying pan and sauté just until the egg sets. Remove from the heat and strain, again extracting as much liquid as possible. (A watery filling will cause the pastry to become soggy.)

METHOD
- To assemble the pie, follow the baklava method on page 153, but instead of the nut filling, spread with the spinach filling. Continue to follow the instructions as for baklava. When completed, cut through the top layers of filo to about halfway through.

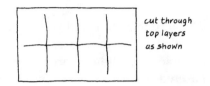

cut through
top layers
as shown

- Bake according to instructions for the baklava recipe.

- Cut into individual pieces, and serve hot or cold.

Egg and Cheese Pie

TYROPITA

Follow the method for spanokopita, but replace the spinach with 1/2 pound grated mature cheese.

Ground Chicken Pie

KOTOPITA

Follow the method for spanokopita, but replace the spinach with 3/4 pound ground chicken.

Puff Pastry Pot

PASTELLE

MAKES 12 PASTELLES

These are neat little individual pies that have been cooked by the Jews of the Middle East for centuries. They are now an established Israeli specialty with two traditional fillings, ground meat or eggplant.

Layered filo pastry can be used, but I prefer thinly rolled puff pastry. The individual pies are about 2 1/2 inches in diameter, with a pastry lid which overhangs the pot. Like filo, when using puff pastry, always prepare the filling first.

Traditionally the pot is molded by hand from a small ball, which produces a better shape than the modern easy way, using a tart tray.

INGREDIENTS

1/2 recipe Spicy Ground Meat (Kiymeh Mashwi Omani for Tatbila) (see page 72) or 2x recipe for Eggplant Dip (Muttabbel/ Baba Ganoush, see page 41)	1 3/4-pound package commercial puff pastry
	2 eggs, beaten

METHOD

- First prepare the filling, then strain and set aside to cool. Preheat the oven to 350°F.

- On a clean, dry work surface, roll out the puff pastry as thinly as you can. To make 12 pies, cut into 24 4-inch squares. Press one square into each depression of a 12-hole tart tin.

- Fill each square, carefully pressing the filling down into the pastry.

- Fit each one with a pastry square lid. Carefully cut around the pie to give it a circular lid which overhangs the pie pot. Remove any extra dough. Be sure that each pie is separated from its neighbor. Brush the tops with the egg.

- Bake for 20 minutes, until the pies are a pale, golden color.

Arab Pizza

LAHMA BI AJEEN

**MAKES 8
LAHMAS**

A dish which usually surprises first-time visitors to the Middle East is *lahma bi ajeen*. This is similar to a pizza in that it consists of a disc of baked pastry with a spicy meat topping. Everyone assumes this dish is simply a modification of the celebrated Italian pizza but actually the origins of this dish are the other way around. It was not the Italians who invented the pizza, it was the Byzantines. At the height of their empire, over 1,000 years ago, they ruled Greece, southern Italy, Syria, and Anatolia (Turkey). This dish was transported from their capital Constantinople (Istanbul) to all parts of their Empire. The name pizza is derived from two Turkish words, *piaz* (onion) and *pita* (bread).

Normally the lahma is a pastry dish of about 6 to 8 inches in diameter, upon which can be put a variety of spicy meat toppings, such as this recipe, which I encountered in Abu Dhabi.

INGREDIENTS

1 recipe khoubiz bread (see page 145), unbaked	1/2 recipe Spicy Ground Meat (Kiymeh Mashwi Omani for Tatbila) (see page 72) (optional)

METHOD

■ Prepare the bread as on page 145 but bake for only 4 or 5 minutes. Turn over and spread with the Spicy Ground Meat, if desired. Bake for another 4 to 5 minutes. This dish can also be grilled, in which case cut the cooking time in half.

Miniature Pizzas

S'FINAH

**MAKES ABOUT
20 S'FINAHS**

A tiny and rather elegant version of lahma bi ajeen is found all over the Levant and the Gulf. Make these exactly as the lahmas (above) but make the disc size no more than 3 inches in diameter. I encountered one clever variation of *s'finah* where the disc was given a slightly convex shape, and a quail's egg was broken on top of the filling and baked.

MEAT DISHES

▲▲▲▲▲▲▲▲▲▲▲▲▲▲▲▲▲▲

When man first began to farm in the Fertile Crescent nearly 10,000 years ago, sheep and goats were bred for both fleece and meat. The domestication of cattle did not take place until some 3,000 years later, and the ancient Turks seem to have pioneered this development. Pork has never been a popular meat in the Middle East although small wild pigs undoubtedly existed. But the Jewish kosher rules formulated thousands of years ago forbade its consumption. Then with the rise of Islam in the seventh century A.D. the pig was considered to be unclean, its flesh the carrier of disease, and an orthodox Moslem (like an orthodox Jew) may not consume any part of the pig. The origins of this taboo are obscure. Lack of cleanliness and disease are not satisfactory reasons, for pork has been the primary meat of the Far East for millennia. The true answer may lie in the fact that pigs, being rooters, simply did not thrive in desert conditions. The few that did, apart from being scarce, may well have been diseased.

The most popular meats in the Middle East are mutton or goat, lamb being a luxury for a special occasion. Beef is permitted and enjoyed, although cattle, oxen, or buffalo are uncommon. Pork is eaten by the Christian communities and offal is popular with everyone. Jews are not permitted to eat rabbit, or any meat cooked or served with dairy products. The Iranians, on the other hand, have developed a style of cooking in which meat is marinated in yogurt.

My selection of recipes includes lamb, beef, veal, pork, and rabbit cooked in a wide variety of methods which include skewered kebabs, ground meat, a number of stews or casseroles, and grilled or fried items. But the dish which everyone associates with the Middle East is whole roast lamb (khouzi) and the recipes for this, and for the smaller leg, are a must for all cooks.

THE KEBAB

Perfected in ancient Turkey, kebabs are now a familiar favorite the world over, and they come in a variety of shapes and sizes. Traditionally, they are made from meat marinated in a mixture of oil and spices, which are then cubed to bite-size pieces, or pounded with a mortar and pestle and shaped on the skewer. The marinade not only gives flavor but tenderizes the meat, which, in the arid Middle East, tends to be tough and stringy. In Western countries meat is very juicy and succulent so the marinade process is for flavor only. We can also be more adventurous with our choice of meat as well—lamb, beef, veal, pork, duck, and chicken can all be used.

Liver, kidneys, and heart can also be cooked as kebabs. Seafood and fish are excellent and, with a little ingenuity, the vegetarian need not be left out. Firm vegetables such as potato, carrot, zucchini, cauliflower, etc., can be marinated in cubes, then cooked or mashed, spiced and shaped, then grilled.

The best flavor is achieved over charcoal but an indoor oven/grill produces results nearly as good.

Marinated Grilled Meat on a Skewer

SHASHLIK KEBAB

SERVES 4

Simple to make and visually attractive, shashlik is a tasty combination of skewered, marinated meat and vegetables, originating from Armenia, but found all over the Middle East. It is a healthy dish, being low in calories, and high in protein and vitamins (especially if you eat the garnish salad).

Serve as a mezzeh item or as a starter on a bed of lettuce topped with mustard greens and parsley, accompanied by lemon or lime wedges and chile sauce (harissa) (see page 37) or yogurt (see page 24). Shashlik makes a fine entrée if served with rice (chellow) (see page 139) and pita bread (see page 146). Traditionally, the meat is goat or mutton, but lamb, pork, or veal may be substituted. But best of all is top-quality beef. For a change, try large prawns or chicken breast (cook these for less time than for meat).

INGREDIENTS

1 pound topside of beef or 1-inch-thick fillet or sirloin steak	1 teaspoon ground cumin
1 red bell pepper	1/2 teaspoon powdered cassia bark or cinnamon
1 green bell pepper	6 tablespoons red wine
1 large onion	1 tablespoon lemon juice
4 green chiles (optional)	2 teaspoons tomato purée
4 cloves garlic (optional)	1/2 teaspoon minced garlic
4 tablespoons olive oil	

METHOD

■ To make the marinade, thoroughly combine the oil, cumin, cassia bark or cinnamon, wine, lemon juice, tomato purée, and garlic in a bowl.

■ Trim any gristle or fat from the meat and cut into 20 cubes a minimum size of 1 inch each.

■ Add the meat to the marinade, then cover with plastic wrap and refrigerate for at least 6 hours (a maximum of 24).

■ Cut the red bell pepper into 8 1-inch diamond or square shapes. Do the same with the green bell pepper. Separate the layers of the onion and cut 20 pieces to the same shape as the peppers.

■ Preheat the oven to 350°F. Thread the ingredients on each skewer as follows: onion, meat, green bell pepper, meat, onion, red bell pepper, meat, onion, green bell pepper, meat, onion, red bell pepper, meat, onion. Add a clove of garlic and/or one green chile, if desired, onto each skewer. Be sure that all the items are close together but not squashed.

■ Place the skewers onto a wire rack and the rack onto a baking tray to catch the drippings. Baste the skewers with the marinade.

■ Cook for 8 to 10 minutes for rare meat, 10 to 15 for medium, and 15 or more for well done. Or you can cook under the broiler at medium heat with the rack at the lowest level for the same times, or cook over charcoal.

Meatballs

KOFTA

These are a type of kebab made from ground meat mixed with herbs and spices, which is shaped into balls and baked or fried and enjoyed nearly everywhere in the Middle East. The *kofta* is a favorite dish in India, undoubtedly taken there by Arab and Moslem invaders. In the Middle East, *koftas* are more likely to be served without a sauce, but with a selection of salads, dips, and bread.

An Arab variation of this dish is called *lahmah-kafta bil karaz* where the lamb is ground, rolled out to cherry-size balls, then grilled to a dark color. These are served in a gravy with firm, sour black local cherries. For the gravy, use the sauce recipe on page 70.

INGREDIENTS

1 1/2 pounds topside of beef or lean leg of lamb	1 tablespoon chopped fresh fenugreek leaves (optional)
2 to 6 cloves garlic, chopped (optional)	1 tablespoon chopped cilantro
1 to 3 teaspoons baharat (see page 19)	4 fresh chiles, chopped (optional)
2 teaspoons dried mint	1/2 teaspoon aromatic salt (see page 23)

METHOD

■ Trim any fat or gristle from the meat and cut into pieces suitable for grinding.

■ In a large bowl, mix all the ingredients together, then grind in a meat grinder or food processor to a fine, well-blended, sticky texture. You can achieve the same texture pounding by hand, but this is a lot of work.

■ Divide the mixture into 4 portions, then subdivide into another 6 to obtain a total of 24 equal portions. Roll into balls.

■ Preheat the oven to 325°F. Place the koftas on a baking sheet for 15 minutes. Or you can grill or barbecue them. Serve with rice and relishes such as dukkah (page 39).

Ground Meat and Cracked Wheat Paste

KIBBEH

Kibbeh is a mixture of ground meat, cracked wheat (bulgur), onion, and spices. It originated thousands of years ago in the Fertile Crescent and to this day it is regarded as the national dish of both Lebanon and Syria. Simple in concept, it has many variations, particularly in the spices used. The Iraqi versions are called koubbah, and in Armenia as keuftas, which are filled with pork. Egyptian variations are made from coarsely ground rice instead of bulgur and are called hamda, and ancient Jewish variations are made from matzo (ground bread). It is also used as a stuffing in vegetables (see page 112). Serve all the kibbeh varieties with a salad, plain yogurt, and khoubiz bread.

Basic Kibbeh

SERVES 4 AS
A SIDE DISH

INGREDIENTS

1/2 cup bulgur	1/4 cup chopped onion
1/2 pound lean leg of lamb	vegetable oil for deep-frying

METHOD

■ Rinse and strain the bulgur.

■ Remove the lamb from the bone, trim away all the fat and gristle, and cut the lamb into chunks.

■ In a bowl, mix the lamb, moist bulgur, and the onion together, then pulse it in a food processor until a paste-like texture is obtained.

■ Scrape this mixture out onto a clean work surface. It should be somewhat sticky, but this makes it a bit tricky to shape. Keep a bowl of warm water nearby and rinse your fingers occasionally. This will help keep the kibbeh balls smooth.

■ Roll into balls or football shapes, and deep-fry for 10 minutes. Drain on paper towels and keep warm until ready to serve.

Ground Meat in a Kibbeh Shell

KIBBEYETS

SERVES 4

The most intriguing use of kibbeh is as a casing around a different ground meat filling. This Syrian recipe has been handed down from mother to daughter for countless generations. The woman who gave it to me explained that in her grandmother's day the eligibility of potential wives was determined by their ability to produce this dish. Its center should be soft and succulent and its outside crust should be crackling crisp. Deep-frying produces the best results.

INGREDIENTS

1/2 pound fillet steak, trimmed and boned leg of lamb, pork (Armenian), or veal	1 teaspoon baharat (see page 19)
	1 teaspoon salt
4 tablespoons clarified butter	1 recipe kibbeh (page 68)
1/4 cup minced onion	vegetable oil for deep-frying
1/4 cup pine nuts	

METHOD

■ To make the filling, trim all the fat and gristle from the meat of your choice. Cut into chunks to enable it to be ground more easily. Place it in a meat grinder or food processor and grind until a sticky paste is achieved.

■ In a skillet or wok, heat the clarified butter and sauté the onion for about 5 minutes. Add the ground meat and sauté for 10 minutes.

■ Grind the pine nuts in a food processor and add them, the baharat, and salt to the meat mixture. Combine thoroughly and then place in a strainer and set aside to cool.

■ To make the kibbeh shells, proceed to the formation stage of the kibbeh recipe on page 68. Divide the paste into 12 equal portions (of about ping-pong ball size). Using a bowl of warm water, keep your hands clean and the meatball smooth. Have the cold filling at hand.

■ Hold one ball in one hand, then poke the index finger of your other hand into the ball and work it gently around until you have made a thin-shelled pouch about the size of a tennis ball. If it breaks, start again, but persevere until you succeed .

■ Carefully spoon the filling into the shell about two-thirds full, then press the shell down to close. Carefully shape it to a rounded cylinder or cone.

■ Preheat a deep-fryer to 330 to 340°F and place 4 of the kibbeyets in the hot oil. Deep-fry about 6 to 8 minutes, until the case is crispy and golden brown.

69

Olive-Studded Meatballs

ZAYTUN MECHOUI

SERVES 4

This decorative and unusual dish is unique to Tunisia. I am not certain of its origins, nor was the chef who showed me his method of making the dish, but he assured me it was a dish which had been a favorite of the Tunisian sultans and their courts. The dish is served as an entrée consisting of several meatballs per person. These are made by pressing halved, pitted olives onto meatballs, then dipping them in flour, eggs, and breadcrumbs, and finally deep-frying them. They are served with a spicy, tomato-based sauce and are garnished with rings of black and green olives, and fresh oregano. Reflecting the ancient Carthaginian link which Tunis has with Sicily, this dish goes exceedingly well with rigatoni or fettucini, especially with a topping of Parmesan cheese and fresh herbs. It is best to make the sauce before the meatballs, either keeping it warm or allowing it to cool (it freezes well), then reheating as required.

INGREDIENTS

SAUCE

4 to 6 canned plum tomatoes

1 red bell pepper

2 to 4 cloves garlic

harissa (see page 37) or to taste (optional)

2 tablespoons olive oil

1 cup stock or water

4 eggs, divided

1 1/2 pounds sirloin steak

4 to 6 cloves garlic, chopped

3/4 cup minced onion

1 teaspoon freshly ground black pepper

1/2 teaspoon aromatic salt (see page 23)

1 tablespoon minced cilantro

3/4 pound green olives, pitted and halved

all-purpose flour

dry breadcrumbs

vegetable oil for deep-frying

black and green olive rings

fresh oregano

METHOD

■ To make the sauce, purée the tomato, bell pepper, garlic, and harissa, if desired, in a blender or food processor. In a skillet or wok, sauté the purée in the hot oil for 5 minutes, then add the stock or water. Simmer until ready to serve with the meatballs, or set aside.

■ In a small skillet, fry 2 of the eggs and set aside to cool. (Eggs are more effective as binding agents when cold.)

■ Trim all the fat and gristle from the steak and cut into chunks.

METHOD

■ Place the meat, garlic, and cold, fried eggs into a food processor and pulse into a coarse paste. Or you can use a hand mincer, putting the mixture through at least twice. Transfer to a large bowl.

■ Add the onion, pepper, salt, and cilantro and combine thoroughly. Divide the mixture into 4 and subdivide into 3's (so that you have 12 equal portions). Roll each portion into a ball and set aside.

■ Press the olive halves onto the surface of the first meatball so that it is sufficiently studded. (Depending on the olive and meatball size, it should take about 12 olive halves for each meatball.) Then roll the meatball in flour and set aside. Continue with the remaining meatballs.

■ In a bowl, beat the remaining 2 eggs. Preheat a deep-fryer to 375°F and, while it is heating, dip each floured meatball in the egg, and then coat in breadcrumbs.

■ Deep-fry 4 meatballs at a time, for 10 to 12 minutes, until they are golden brown. Set aside and keep warm while the second and third batches are cooking.

■ Reheat the sauce, if necessary, and pour it over the meatballs. Serve garnished with olives and oregano.

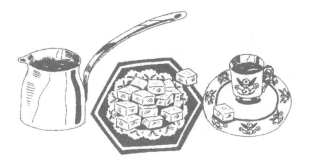

Spicy Ground Meat

KIYMEH MASHWI OMANI

SERVES 4

This dish from the Gulf state of Oman is a combination of cooked ground meat (usually mutton) and several spices. Pronounced keema, this dish clearly owes its origins to India, where a similarly named dish is very popular. More than likely the recipe traveled across the Arabian Sea centuries ago when the early trade routes connected the two regions. Serve with a rice dish and a relish, such as hilbeh (see page 36).

INGREDIENTS

2 teaspoons coriander seeds

1 teaspoon cumin seeds

2 teaspoons green cardamom

1/2 teaspoon caraway

1 teaspoon turmeric

1 teaspoon cayenne

2 tablespoons clarified butter or vegetable oil

6 cloves garlic, chopped

1 2-inch piece ginger, chopped

1 cup minced onion

1 1/2 pounds ground beef, mutton, or lamb

3/4 cup chopped tomatoes

1 tablespoon chopped cilantro

1 teaspoon baharat (see page 19)

salt to taste

METHOD

■ To make the spice paste, mix all the spices with just enough water to make a paste and set aside.

■ In a large skillet or wok, heat the clarified butter or oil and sauté the garlic for 1 minute. Add the ginger and continue to sauté for another minute, then add the onion and continue to cook for about 10 more minutes over medium-high heat.

■ Add the spice paste to the onion and sauté for 2 or 3 minutes. Then add the ground meat and continue to sauté for 10 more minutes.

■ Lower the heat, add the tomato, and simmer for 20 minutes, stirring occasionally.

■ Stir in the cilantro and baharat, and continue to simmer until it is ready to serve. Season with salt.

Ground Meat with Eggs

KIYMAIL YUMURTA

This Turkish ground meat dish is topped off with eggs. Prepare the ground meat as for kiymeh on page 72. After the meat has simmered in the sauce, press it into a pan and break 4 eggs over it, continuing to simmer until the eggs are cooked to your liking. For the best results, finish them off under the grill.

Traditionally this dish would be considerably less spicy, so reduce quantities or omit spices to your taste.

Couscous Meat Stew

SERVES 4

Couscous is described as the national dish of Morocco and it is certainly one of the most well-known North African dishes. To cook the couscous grain, see the recipe on page 133. To cook the stew with couscous, the Moroccans use a couscousière, which is a special double boiler, and if you find that you prepare couscous frequently, one is worth obtaining. Otherwise, use a deep, lidded saucepan of about 8 inches in diameter, and a sieve of the same diameter which fits well without its bottom touching the liquid inside the saucepan.

Two recipes follow, one from Tangiers, and a spicier version from Fez in southern Morocco, using merguez sausage (see page 50) or khlii dried meat, and ras-el-hanout, the special Moroccan spice mixture (see page 19). If you want the hot taste of Tunisia add chiles and harissa to taste.

INGREDIENTS

1 1/2 pounds stewing steak	4 to 6 canned tomatoes
4 tablespoons clarified butter or vegetable oil	1 red bell pepper, stemmed, seeded, and chopped
1 cup chopped onion	freshly ground black pepper and salt to taste
1 teaspoon ground cumin	

METHOD

- Trim the fat and gristle from the meat and cut it into 1 1/2-inch cubes.

- In a skillet or wok, heat the clarified butter or oil and sauté the onion and cumin for 5 minutes. Add the meat and continue to sauté for 10 minutes to seal it.

73

METHOD

■ Transfer this mixture and the tomatoes and red pepper to a saucepan as described above, adding approximately the same volume of boiling water, and bring it to a boil. Lower the heat and simmer for 30 minutes, stirring occasionally.

■ Place the couscous (as described on page 133) into a muslin-lined sieve which fits onto the saucepan with the meat mixture. Put the lid on the sieve and continue to simmer the stew for 20 more minutes. The steam cooks and flavors the couscous. Fluff it up with a fork about every 5 minutes.

■ When the couscous is cooked to your liking, remove it from the muslin liner and carefully mound onto a serving dish. Put it in a warm oven until ready to serve.

■ Season the stew with pepper and salt, then strain it, reserving the liquid and transferring it to a gravy boat.

■ Make a depression in the couscous and nestle the dry stew inside it.

■ To serve, place the dish on the table, allowing the diners to help themselves, and add gravy to taste.

Fez-Style Couscous Meat Stew

SERVES 4

For this spicy variation, follow the preceding recipe, but use a combination of equal parts of steak and merguez or similar sausage (see page 50). This should use about two sausages.

METHOD

■ Trim the steak of any fat and gristle and mix with the sausage meat that has been removed from its casings and chopped.

■ Add 2 to 4 cloves crushed garlic and 1 tablespoon ras-el-hanout (see page 19).

■ Proceed with the instructions for the preceding recipe. Garnish with chopped cilantro.

Slow-Cooked Stew

CHOLENT

SERVES 4

The origins of this dish are a little obscure, but it is to be found in every Jewish household all over the world. It is a dish normally eaten on the Sabbath, when no work, including cooking, is permitted. It was probably originated by the medieval Sephardic Jews of Palestine who took it with them when they migrated to Europe and later the U.S., where over the centuries it became the less spicy dish known as cholent. Both versions have become established as Israeli favorites.

INGREDIENTS

1 1/2 pounds stewing steak	1 1-inch piece ginger, chopped (optional)
1 cup potatoes	2 to 4 teaspoons baharat (see page 19) (optional)
1 cup carrots and/or parsnip and/or turnip	
4 tablespoons vegetable oil	1/2 cup pearl barley or whole wheat
1 to 4 cloves garlic, minced	salt and black pepper to taste
1 cup minced onion	fresh cilantro or parsley, coarsely chopped

METHOD

- Trim the fat and gristle from the meat and cut it into 2-inch cubes.

- Wash and peel the potatoes, then cut into 1 1/2-inch pieces. Place in a bowl of cold water and set aside.

- Wash and peel the carrots, parsnips, and turnips and cut into 1-inch pieces. Add to the potatoes in the bowl of water.

- In a skillet or wok, heat the oil and sauté the garlic for 1 minute. Then add the onion and continue to sauté for 5 or 6 minutes.

- Add the meat and cook about 10 minutes to seal it. Preheat the oven to 375°F.

- Transfer the sautéed meat to a casserole dish, adding the remaining ingredients and combinining them thoroughly. Add approximately the same volume of boiling water. Put the lid on the casserole and place in the oven. Bake for 30 minutes, then check and stir. Reduce the heat to 250°F and bake for 3 or 4 hours. Season with salt and pepper.

- To serve the traditional way, strain off the gravy and place it in a gravy boat. Divide equal quantities of the meat on each of 4 serving plates and arrange the remaining ingredients around the meat. Garnish with cilantro or parsley. This is a meal in itself and needs no side dishes.

Lamb in a Creamy Aromatic Sauce

KORESH OR KORAK

SERVES 4

This dish originated in ancient Persia. Literally meaning "sauce poured over rice," it appears at nearly every meal, and in many guises. The korak is the thicker version, containing meat, poultry, or vegetables, and often dried fruit and nuts. Sometimes yogurt is used and the dish is spiced, but the spicing is subtle and aromatic, never overwhelming and hot. The tastes combine sweet and sour and the textures are soft and crunchy.

INGREDIENTS

1 1/2 pounds leg of lamb	1/2 teaspoon freshly ground black pepper
4 tablespoons clarified butter or vegetable oil	1/2 cup dried apricots, prunes, and/or firm, sour, fresh cherries
1 cup chopped onion	1/2 to 1 teaspoon sumak (optional)
1 teaspoon turmeric	2 to 4 loumi (dried limes)
1 teaspoon powdered cinnamon	aromatic salt to taste (see page 23)
1/3 teaspoon ground cloves	

METHOD

■ Trim the fat and gristle from the lamb and cut into 1 1/2-inch pieces.

■ In a skillet or wok, heat the clarified butter or oil to just below smoking point. Sauté the onions for 5 or 6 minutes, then add the turmeric, cinnamon, cloves, and pepper, sautéing for another 5 minutes.

■ Preheat the oven to 375°F. Transfer the above fried items to a casserole dish and mix in the meat, dried fruit, if being used (but none of the fresh fruit), sumak, if desired, and loumi. Place the casserole in the oven and bake covered for 20 minutes.

■ Remove, check, and stir. Add a little water, if necessary, and return to the oven for 20 more minutes. Remove and stir in any fresh fruit, then return to the oven for a final cooking of 10 minutes, until it is done to your liking. Season with salt. Serve with rice.

Lamb Cooked with Yogurt

LABAN UMMO OR MANSAAF

SERVES 4

This is another very ancient dish. Bedouin tribespeople regarded water as their most precious asset, and it could not always be spared for cooking. Thus, milk was sometimes the cooking medium. Today the dish uses thickened yogurt. It is made in Syria and Lebanon, where it is called laban (yogurt) ummo. In Jordan and the Gulf, virtually the same dish is called mansaaf, and in Palestine it is mansi.

INGREDIENTS

1 1/2 pounds leg of lamb (for laban ummo) or 2 1/2 pounds leg of lamb (for mansaaf)	1 cup stock or water
2 to 4 cloves garlic, chopped	2/3 cup yogurt
3/4 cup chopped onion	1 tablespoon corn flour
1 teaspoon ground allspice	2 tablespoons milk
1 teaspoon baharat (see page 19) (for mansaaf only)	salt to taste
4 tablespoons clarified butter or vegetable oil	1 tablespoon chopped fresh mint and/or cilantro

METHOD

■ Trim the lamb of any fat or gristle and cut to 1 1/2-inch cubes for laban ummo. For mansaaf, trim off as much fat as possible, keeping the leg whole.

■ Preheat the oven to 375°F. Place the lamb, garlic, onion, allspice, baharat, and clarified butter or oil with the stock or water in a large casserole dish. Cover and bake for 20 minutes; check, stir (the laban ummo), and cook for another 20 minutes.

■ While the lamb is baking, mix the yogurt with the corn flour in a saucepan. Whisk vigorously, and cook over medium heat, stirring continuously, until thickened. Add the milk a little at a time.

■ Pour the yogurt mixture over the lamb at the end of the second 20-minute baking period, and season with salt. Return to the oven for at least 10 more minutes or until tender. Garnish with fresh mint and/or cilantro. Serve with a rice dish.

Veal with Apricots

MISHMISHEYA

SERVES 4

This dish is Persian in origin, although it is, in fact, an Algerian recipe. Mishmish means "apricot" in Arabic, but all kinds of dried or fresh fruit can be used. Here fresh apricots are made into a paste and the meat is veal, but it also works very well with pork.

INGREDIENTS

1 1/2 pounds leg of veal or pork	1 teaspoon powdered cinnamon
4 tablespoons clarified butter or vegetable oil	1 teaspoon ground coriander
	1 teaspoon ground cumin
2 cloves garlic, minced	stock or water
1 1-inch piece ginger, minced	2/3 cup fresh apricots or peaches
1 cup minced onion	salt to taste
1 teaspoon ground allspice	1 tablespoon brown sugar (optional)

METHOD

■ Trim all the fat and gristle from the meat and cut it into 1-inch cubes.

■ In a skillet or wok, heat the clarified butter or oil and sauté the garlic for 1 minute. Add the ginger, sauté for another minute, then add the onion and cook for 5 more minutes.

■ In a bowl, mix the allspice, cinnamon, coriander, and cumin with enough water to make a runny paste, then add it to the frying pan. Mix well.

■ Preheat the oven to 375°F. Place the meat and sautéed ingredients into a casserole dish with a little stock or water. Bake covered for 20 minutes. Remove, check, and stir, adding more stock or water, if necessary. Return to oven and cook for another 20 minutes.

■ While the meat is cooking, peel, halve, and pit the apricots or peaches. If the fruit is very soft, mash it with a fork. If firm, use the blender or food processor.

■ Remove the casserole from the oven, and stir in the puréed fruit, salt, and sugar, if desired. Return to the oven for another 10 minutes. Serve with couscous.

Heart, Kidney and Liver Sauté

KIRSHUH

SERVES 4

In all the Arab countries necessity has inspired many tasty ways of using offal. This recipe from Yemen, which is very curry-like in flavor, exemplifies the historical ties of the Yemeni's ancient trading links with India, and its large migrant Indian population. There are no strict rules as to which offal and which spices should be used, so follow this recipe as a guide and adjust ingredients to suit your palate.

INGREDIENTS

1 teaspoon turmeric	6 to 10 cloves garlic, minced
2 teaspoons ground coriander	1 2-inch piece ginger, minced
1 teaspoon ground cumin	1 cup minced onion
1 teaspoon baharat (see page 19)	4-6 canned plum tomatoes, chopped
1 1/2 pounds heart, kidney, or liver, and/or lamb, calf, beef, pork, or poultry	1 tablespoon chopped cilantro
4 tablespoons vegetable oil	salt and black pepper to taste

METHOD

■ To make the spice paste, in a mixing bowl combine the spices together with enough water to make a paste, and set aside.

■ Trim the meat of any fat and gristle and cut into bite-size cubes.

■ In a skillet or wok, heat the oil and sauté the garlic for 1 minute, then add the ginger and sauté for another minute. Add the spice paste and cook for 2 more minutes, and then add the onion, and finally the meat.

■ Sauté for 10 more minutes, adding a little water to prevent sticking.

■ Add the tomatoes and cilantro, season with salt and pepper, and simmer for 10 to 15 minutes. Serve hot with rice or couscous.

Spicy, Marinated, Roast Rabbit

ARNHAB CHERMOULA

SERVES 4

Chermoula or tchermita is a paste made from red and gold spices bound with olive oil, onion, and garlic. It is used as a marinade base for fish, poultry, meat, or game which is subsequently grilled. A visitor to the ancient Moroccan markets—the medinas—is bound to be drawn to the open-air braziers of the street food traders who take some meat pieces from a marinade, deftly skewer them, and grill them while you wait.

The ingredients will vary from trader to trader and day to day. I have had fish, chicken, pigeon, rabbit, mutton, and goat, and after one rather chewy, highly spiced occasion, I found I had just eaten camel!

INGREDIENTS

1 3- to 3 1/2-pound whole rabbit, skinned and gutted	1 recipe chermoula (see page 19)
4 to 6 tablespoons vinegar	watercress, parsley, and other herbs

METHOD

■ Wash the rabbit inside and out, dry thoroughly, and remove fat and membrane. Make small slashes in the deep flesh with the tip of a sharp knife.

■ Rub in the vinegar and let the rabbit rest for 1 to 2 hours.

■ Rub the chermoula marinade thoroughly into the meat, then cover and refrigerate for at least 6 hours (a maximum of 24).

■ Cook the rabbit on a spit over charcoal for 15-25 minutes, checking it regularly so that it doesn't overcook. Or you can cook the rabbit in your oven, using either a spit rotisserie or a wire rack on a baking sheet. Preheat the oven to 350°F. Shake off the excess marinade, but reserve it and set aside. Put the whole rabbit onto a skewer or oven rack (with a baking sheet beneath to catch the drips), then place in the oven and roast for between 20 and 30 minutes, basting with excess marinade in the early stages. Check for doneness during the final minutes of cooking, removing from the oven when it is to your liking.

■ Either serve whole on a central serving dish, or cut it into portions. Garnish with watercress, parsley, and other herbs of your choice. Serve with rice or couscous, and spicy dips such as harissa and dukkah (see pages 37 and 39).

Whole Roasted Lamb

KHOUZI OR M'CHOUI

SERVES 16 TO 20

No cookbook on Middle Eastern cookery would be complete without a recipe for roasted whole lamb, the traditional Arab ceremonial dish. When I was quite young, a middle-aged friend used to thrill me with tales of feasts held especially for him when he was in Arabia negotiating with villagers over oil rights. Invariably roast lamb was the featured entrée, and as guest of honor he would be expected to eat two great delicacies—the eyes and the testicles. He never got over his squeamishness, but eat them he did, and with apparent gusto, for he could have caused enormous offense if he had refused.

In Morocco the dish is called m'choui (from the Arabic word to grill). The carcass is marinated inside and out with spicy chermoula paste. It is given as an option here.

For an everyday version, use one 3 1/2- to 4-pound leg of lamb on the bone, and cook it at the same temperature for 1 1/2 to 2 hours.

To calculate the cooking time of a whole carcass, use the formula for a leg joint, 1/2 hour per one pound. Remember it has four leg joints so divide the total carcass weight by 4, then multiply by 1/2 hour. An 8-pound carcass will take 1 hour to cook, and a 12-pound carcass 1 1/2 hours. These are minimum cooking times and the lamb will be pink.

INGREDIENTS

1 cup olive or vegetable oil	1 8- to 12-pound lamb, oven-ready
4 tablespoons baharat (see page 19) (for khouzi)	2 tablespoons za'atar (see page 20)
1 recipe chermoula (see page 19) (for m'choui)	2 tablespoons chopped cilantro or parsley

METHOD

■ In a bowl, mix the oil and spices together for either coating, then rub into the lamb. Set aside any unused sauce.

■ Preheat the oven to 325°F. Place the lamb on an oven rack with a roasting pan underneath to catch drips.

■ Calculate your cooking time at 1/2 hour per 1 pound of meat (so roughly 1 to 1 1/2 hours). Turn and baste with extra coating sauce every 20 to 30 minutes.

METHOD

■ Because of the variations in oven temperatures you must check on the tenderness of your lamb by pricking the meat with the tip of a sharp knife. When it is cooked to your taste, let it rest for 20 to 30 minutes in a warm oven.

■ To serve, place the whole lamb on a bed of rice, sprinkling on the za'atar and cilantro or parsley.

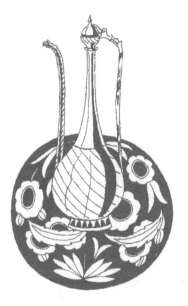

POULTRY DISHES

▲▲▲▲▲▲▲▲▲▲▲▲▲▲▲▲▲

By 8000 B.C., the earliest settlers of the Fertile Crescent had domesticated the wild chicken, a descendant of the Indian jungle fowl, breeding it for eggs and meat. Today it is popular roasted, with or without stuffing, and is both casseroled and stewed. Less conventional cooking methods include frying balls of ground chicken or puréeing it with wheat. But the most remarkable chicken dish in the Middle Eastern repertoire is *pilich dolmasi*, said to have been created for Ottoman rulers; it is made of ground meat enclosed within a whole chicken skin and baked. Another festive dish, *faisanjan*, first created in the royal Persian court, features peacock, or duck nowadays. Duck does not figure largely in traditional Middle Eastern cookery, although the ancient Egyptians bred them for the tables of the rich. Today duck is more readily available, although as in the West, it is relatively expensive.

Small birds of all kinds are also consumed in the Middle East. Sparrows, finches, linnets, and larks are caught and grilled as they have been for thousands of years. So too are pheasant, partridge, grouse, quail, dove, and pigeon.

Goose has been an Egyptian specialty since Pharaonic times, and it is now bred in modern Israel for export. A rather scrawny, small turkey is raised in Turkey although, in fact, turkey did not originate there. The Turkish name for it is *hindi* (or Indian), probably because turkeys originated in America, at first *thought* to be India. How we came to call it "turkey" is speculation. Perhaps an English ambassador on a visit to the Ottoman court feasted on turkey. He may have been shown the strutting fowl with its curious gobble-gobble conversation and its pompous, puffed-up appearance. In his explanation to the English court, the ambassador may have likened the bird to the sultan himself—and the name stuck.

Roast Chicken

DJEJ MECHOUI

SERVES 4

Roast chicken is as popular in the Middle East as it is in the West. There are many variations, ranging from simple and unadorned to heavily spiced and stuffed with couscous.

In this recipe I have provided a basic roast chicken with 2 marinades, one minimally spiced, and the other more heavily spiced in a recipe from the Yemen. In the Middle East the cooking would be over charcoal, but the instructions here are for roasting.

INGREDIENTS

1 3 1/2-pound chicken, oven-ready

MILD MARINADE
3/4 cup olive oil

4 tablespoons fresh lemon juice

2 teaspoons aromatic salt (see page 23)

1 teaspoon freshly ground black pepper

SPICY MARINADE
1/2 teaspoon turmeric

1 teaspoon cumin

1 teaspoon coriander

1 teaspoon baharat (see page 19)

2 teaspoons dried mint

METHOD

■ Make sure the cavity is empty, then place the chicken in a roasting pan.

■ In a bowl, combine all the ingredients of one of the marinades and rub all over the chicken. Cover and refrigerate at least 2 hours (a maximum of 24 hours), basting occasionally.

■ Preheat the oven to 375°F. Place the chicken onto an oven rack over a roasting pan, basting with the marinade. Pour off the excess marinade and set aside.

■ Roast for 20 minutes per pound, basting every 15 minutes with the marinade.

■ For the final 10 minutes, bake the chicken at 425°F.

■ Remove the chicken from the oven, and let it rest for 15 minutes before serving.

Couscous-Stuffed Roast Chicken with Red Sauce

DJEJ M'AHMAR

SERVES 4

In this Algerian version of a favoriate North African dish, the chicken is glazed with honey and the couscous contains sultanas. The result is a delicious, savory-sweet combination served with a lovely red sauce, the m'ahmar.

INGREDIENTS

3/4 cup precooked couscous	1 teaspoon cumin seeds
1/4 cup pine nuts	1 cup chicken stock or water
1/4 cup sultanas	2 tablespoons tomato purée
1/4 cup whole almonds	salt
Chicken and marinade of choice as for Roast Chicken (page 84)	20 saffron threads
4 tablespoons clarified butter	2 tablespoons warm milk
2 teaspoons paprika	4 tablespoons clear honey

METHOD

■ To make the stuffing, combine the couscous, pine nuts, sultanas, and almonds in a bowl, then stuff the chicken.

■ Follow the recipe for Roast Chicken (page 84) through the roasting process.

■ Meanwhile, make the sauce. In a large skillet or wok, heat the clarified butter and sauté the paprika and cumin seeds for 1 minute. Add the stock or water and the tomato purée and season with salt. Simmer for 30 minutes until the liquid is reduced by one-third.

■ In a small bowl, add the saffron to the milk and leave for 10 minutes, or until the milk has turned a golden yellow, then add it to sauce.

■ When the roasting process is almost complete, glaze the chicken with the honey and roast for a final 10 minutes.

■ Remove from the oven and allow to rest for 15 minutes, before transferring to a serving platter. Pour the hot sauce over the chicken, or serve it in a gravy boat.

Roast Chicken Stuffed with Rice

DAJAJ M'ASHI

SERVES 4

This recipe is from the Saudi Arabian capital city of Riyadh.

INGREDIENTS

1 tablespoon vegetable oil	1 teaspoon powdered cinnamon
1/4 cup chopped onion	1/4 cup chopped almonds
2 to 4 cloves garlic, chopped	Chicken and marinade of choice as for Roast Chicken (page 84)
3/4 cup cooked basmati rice	

METHOD

- To make the stuffing, in a skillet or wok heat the oil and sauté the onion and garlic. Transfer to a bowl and mix thoroughly with the rice, cinnamon, and almonds, then stuff the chicken.

- Follow the recipe for Roast Chicken (page 84).

Stuffed, Filleted Ground Chicken

PILICH DOLMASI

SERVES 4

This is a dish devised in sixteenth-century Turkey to gratify the opulent Ottoman sultans. The chicken appears to be a normal roast chicken and, without giving the game away, carving should take place in front of your guests. This chicken has no bones and the meat is ground and combined with a mixture of nuts, herbs, and spices, so it carves into neat slices.

The only difficulty in preparing this dish lies in removing the chicken skin in one piece. You can do it yourself, but it is tricky and it is easy to tear a hole in it. Ask your butcher to do it for you. If there are a few small holes in the skin, smooth them down against the ground meat.

INGREDIENTS

1 1 1/2- to 2-pound chicken with skin	1 teaspoon ground allspice
flesh, liver, kidney, and heart of the chicken	1/2 teaspoon aromatic salt (see page 23)
1 cup chicken breast	1/2 teaspoon freshly ground black pepper
1 cup leg of veal	1/2 cup olive oil
1/4 cup pine nuts	2 tablespoons lemon juice
2 to 4 cloves garlic, chopped	1 teaspoon aromatic salt (see page 23)
1/4 cup chopped onion	1 teaspoon paprika
1 teaspoon powdered cinnamon	

METHOD

■ Remove the chicken skin or have your butcher do it and set aside.

■ Remove the flesh from the bone, trim any fat and gristle, then cut the meat in pieces suitable for grinding.

■ Prepare the chicken breast (discarding the skin) and the veal as above.

■ To make the stuffing, put all the meats twice through a fine grinder with all but the remaining 4 basting ingredients. Or pulse to a coarse texture in a food processor, then mix well by hand.

■ Hold the chicken skin open and carefully fill it with stuffing.. Don't overfill the skin—leave enough room to fold the openings over and to shape it back to that of a bird. There should be a little stuffing left over which can be frozen for later use.

■ To make the basting liquid, combine the oil, lemon juice, salt, and paprika in a bowl.

METHOD

■ Preheat the oven to 375°F. Place the chicken in a roasting pan in the oven and baste occasionally with one-third of the basting mixture. Roast for 15 minutes.

■ Remove from the oven, and turn the chicken upside down. Baste with one-third more of the basting mixture, and roast another 15 minutes.

■ Repeat, turning the chicken back the right way up, using the remaining basting mixture. Cook for a final 15 to 20 minutes.

■ Remove the chicken from the oven and let it rest for about 10 minutes.

■ Transfer to a large serving platter for carving. Serve with rice and vegetables.

Fried Ground Chicken Balls

KOFTIT FERAKH

SERVES 4

Like their meat counterparts, these ground chicken balls are popular all over the Middle East. This version is from Syria, where they grind pine nuts, cumin seeds, and fresh herbs with the meat. In the Gulf they add chile and turmeric, and in Iran they use pistachio nuts instead of pine nuts to make *kufta morgi*. In Turkey the dish is called *tavak koftesi*, and nuts are replaced by breadcrumbs. The chicken balls vary from the size of a cherry to the size of a baseball. To obtain exactly equal sizes, divide the mixture into 4, then into 4 again for large-size balls, and into 4 yet again for cherry-size balls.

INGREDIENTS

1 1/2 pounds chicken breast	1 teaspoon ground cumin
2 to 4 cloves garlic (optional)	2 to 4 fresh green chiles (optional)
1/4 cup chopped onion	1 tablespoon chopped cilantro

METHOD

■ Remove the skin, bones, and fat from the chicken and cut into workable pieces. Then grind the chicken pieces, garlic, if desired, onion, cumin, chiles, if desired, and cilantro together by hand in a fine meat grinder twice, or pulse in a food processor until you have a well-blended, somewhat glutinous mixture.

■ Heat oven or deep-fryer to 375°F. Divide the mixture as described above, and cook for no more than 10 minutes (about 7 or 8 minutes for cherry-size balls). Drain on paper towels.

■ Serve with salad, dips, and bread.

Chicken with Dates and Honey

TAGINE DJEJ BIL TAMAR WA ASSAL

SERVES 4

The *tagine* is the ubiquitous Berber slow-cooked stew. Tagine is also the name of the container in which the stew is cooked, over charcoal. It is in two parts: the base is a wide, round, earthenware dish, and on top of this sits a tight-fitting conical lid.

The stew itself can include any ingredients of the cook's choice and whatever the contents, the cooking is simple. Add plenty of water and simmer on low heat until it is juicy, tender, and the liquid is reduced.

This particular recipe is a northern Moroccan combination of chicken, spices, nuts, honey, and dates; its sweet, sour, and savory flavor and soft yet crunchy texture reflects a Persian influence.

INGREDIENTS

1 1/2 pounds chicken	2 cups boiling water
4 tablespoons clarified butter or vegetable oil	2 or 3 bay leaves
1 cup chopped onion	12 to 16 fresh dates, seeded and halved
1 clove garlic, chopped	4 tablespoons whole almonds
2 teaspoons la kama (see page 19)	2 tablespoons honey
1 teaspoon cumin seeds	aromatic salt to taste (see page 23)

METHOD

■ Remove the skin, bones, and fat from the chicken and cut into bite-size cubes.

■ In a heavy saucepan, heat the clarified butter or oil and sauté the onion, garlic, la kama, and cumin for 15 minutes.

■ Add the water and bay leaves, and simmer, uncovered, for 30 minutes until the liquid has reduced by about one-third.

■ Add the chicken meat and continue to simmer for 20 minutes, stirring occasionally, and adding a little water if it becomes too dry.

■ Add the dates, almonds, honey, and salt and continue to simmer for up to 10 more minutes. Serve with couscous or rice.

Sesame-Coated Chicken Pieces

SIMSIM DAJ

SERVES 4

This recipe may have originated in Jerusalem centuries ago. It has evolved today into a popular Israeli snack or entrée, and the modern oven makes it simple to cook. The secret of success lies in roasting the sesame seeds, in removing the chicken skin, and in marinating the chicken for a long time.

INGREDIENTS

4 6-ounce chicken breasts	1 teaspoon aromatic salt (see page 23)
8 tablespoons sunflower oil	1/4 cup sesame seeds
4 tablespoons tahini (see page 20)	lemon wedges
1 teaspoon paprika	fresh chopped parsley
2 cloves garlic, puréed, or 2 teaspoons garlic powder	

METHOD

■ Remove the skin, bones, and fat from the chicken and cut each breast into four strips.

■ To make the marinade, in a bowl mix the oil, tahini, paprika, garlic, and salt to achieve a smooth paste, about the consistency of ketchup.

■ Place the chicken and marinade into a glass or ceramic bowl, mix well, cover, and refrigerate at least 6 hours (a maximum of 24 hours).

■ Preheat the oven to 325°F. Spread the sesame seeds on a baking sheet and bake for 10 minutes. Remove and set aside to cool (keep the oven on). When cool, return some seeds to the baking sheet.

■ Be sure that the chicken pieces are well coated with marinade, and arrange them one by one on the sesame seed-covered baking sheet. Pour more marinade over the chicken and sprinkle the remaining sesame seeds over the top of the chicken.

■ Bake in the oven for 20 minutes. Garnish with lemon wedges and parsley. Serve with potatoes and vegetables or salad, bread, and dips.

Circassian Chicken

CERKEZ TAVAGU

SERVES 4

Strips of cooked chicken breast are encased in a thick, pink, walnut-based purée. The dish originates in the most northern of our Middle Eastern countries, Georgia, but is also found in Armenia and Turkey. It reflects the Caucasian love of walnuts and olive oil, and puréed textures. It is rich and attractive and is delicious served cold as a mezzeh dish, as a salad, or as a hot entrée.

INGREDIENTS

1 1/2 pounds chicken breast	1 red bell pepper, stemmed, seeded, and chopped
4 tablespoons olive oil	1/3 cup cream cheese
1/2 cup walnuts, shelled	2 teaspoons paprika
2 slices white or wheat bread, crusts removed	2 tablespoons walnut or hazelnut oil
2 cups chicken stock	salt and freshly ground black pepper to taste
1/4 cup chopped carrot	fresh chopped parsley
2 to 4 cloves garlic, chopped	black olives
1/2 cup chopped onion	strips of red bell pepper

METHOD

■ Remove the skin, bones, and fat from the chicken and cut into strips averaging 2 x 1/2 inches.

■ In a wok or large frying pan, heat the olive oil and sauté the chicken strips for about 10 minutes, ensuring that they are evenly and thoroughly cooked. Set aside.

■ In a blender or food processor, grind the walnuts and bread to a fine crumbly mixture by pulsing in short bursts to minimize the chance of over-heating and making the nuts oily.

■ In a large stockpot, bring the stock to a boil and add the carrot, garlic, onion, and bell pepper. Lower the heat and simmer for 10 minutes until the vegetables are soft. Strain (reserving the stock) and purée.

■ In a mixing bowl, combine the walnut-breadcrumb mixture with the vegetable purée and enough of the stock to make a thick creamy texture. Add the cream cheese, paprika, walnut or hazelnut oil, salt, and pepper.

METHOD

■ To serve this dish cold, allow the purée to cool completely and then mix half of it with all the chicken, putting it into an oval serving dish. Spread the remaining paste over the top and garnish with parsley, olives, and bell pepper. Serve with a green salad and pita bread.

■ To serve hot, slowly heat the purée in the wok or large frying pan, stirring to prevent sticking. Add the chicken and some stock, as needed, garnish, and serve hot with rice and vegetables.

Siman Bil Kibbeh

QUAIL STUFFED WITH GROUND MEAT AND BULGUR

SERVES 4

The Egyptians are especially fond of stuffed, baked, or boiled small birds. This recipe for quail stuffed with kibbeh is typically Egyptian, and comes from Egypt's best restaurant, the El Nile Rôtisserie in the Nile Hilton Hotel, Cairo.

INGREDIENTS

8 6-ounce quails, oven-ready	6 tablespoons olive oil
1 recipe kibbeh (see page 68)	1 tablespoon lemon juice
1 teaspoon roasted cumin seeds	1 teaspoon aromatic salt (see page 23)
1 teaspoon bahar (see page 19)	

METHOD

■ Preheat the oven to 325°F. Make sure that the cavities of the quails are clean.

■ In a bowl, combine the kibbeh mixture with the cumin and bahar, then spoon into the quails. Seal by pulling the end flap over the opening.

■ Place the quails in a roasting pan. In a small bowl, combine the oil, lemon juice, and salt, and use to baste the quails.

■ Bake in the oven for about 10 minutes. Then, using the basting mixture in the pan, baste and cook for another 10 minutes.

■ Serve two per person with rice and vegetables.

Casseroled Turkey with Chestnuts

KESTANEZI HINDI GUVECH

SERVES 4

This dish, with its chestnut accompaniment, is quite delicious. Serve with rice and/or vegetables.

INGREDIENTS

1 1/2 pounds turkey breast and/or thigh	1 teaspoon paprika
4 tablespoons vegetable oil	1 teaspoon powdered cinnamon
1 cup chopped onions	1 cup water or chicken stock
2 cloves garlic, chopped	1 pound 2 ounces chestnuts, peeled
4–6 canned plum tomatoes, chopped	aromatic salt to taste (see page 23)
1 red bell pepper, stemmed, seeded, and minced	freshly ground black pepper to taste

METHOD

■ Preheat the oven to 375°F. Remove the skin, bones, and fat from the turkey and cut into bite-size pieces.

■ In a large skillet or wok, heat the oil and sauté the onion and garlic for about 10 minutes.

■ Transfer the sautéed mixture, turkey, tomatoes, bell pepper, paprika, and cinnamon to a casserole dish. Add the water or stock and bake, covered, for 20 minutes.

■ Meanwhile, prepare the chestnuts. If fresh, pierce the skins, lightly grill them, and then peel. If canned, use the liquid as well. If you can get them (and they are available in this form all year) use vacuum-packed, peeled, and cooked chestnuts.

■ Check the casserole and add more water or stock, if necessary; stir in the chestnuts. Bake for another 20 minutes.

■ Remove the casserole and season with salt and pepper. Test the turkey for doneness. It should be tender enough to serve.

Duck in a Sweet and Sour Sauce

FAISINJAN KORESH

SERVES 4

At the time of the Shahs of Persia, peacock would have been the subject of this dish. At court the whole cooked peacock would be presented on a sea of bright red pomegranate seeds surrounded by saffron yellow rice on a huge jewel-encrusted gold serving dish, adorned with a swaying forest of peacock feathers. A procession of servants would parade dozens of these colorful identical dishes before the assembled all-male court to the accompanying cacophony of reed instruments and drums. At a given sign the marching and trumpeting would cease, the dishes would be held on high, and the Shah would bless them. Then they would be set down amongst the courtiers, who would devour their faisinjan with relish. The Shah would sit on his throne observing but not partaking—his own *faisinjan* would come later, out of sight of the court, tested for poison, and in the private company of his harem.

Today faisinjan is still served at special occasions such as weddings and other times of celebration, and when a special guest visits the household. However, now the main ingredient is wild game such as pheasant or wild duck. The sourness of the pomegranate contrasts with game extremely well. I have modified this dish a little by using domestic duckling which I then roast rather than casserole. This allows you to get rid of most of the fat. The thick sauce is added at the end and if you can't get fresh pomegranate, or if you don't like it, substitute unsweetened red currants.

INGREDIENTS

1 3 1/2- to 4-pound whole duckling or small duck, oven ready	2 to 4 tablespoons pomegranate seeds, dry
4 tablespoons duck fat	1 cup water
2 cloves garlic, minced	1 to 3 tablespoons brown sugar
1 cup chopped onion	lemon juice to taste (optional)
1 teaspoon ground cumin	1/2 cup fresh pomegranate seeds, or unsweetened red currants
1 teaspoon turmeric	
1 teaspoon powdered cinnamon	2 tablespoons chopped pistachio nuts
1/2 cup ground almonds	2 tablespoons chopped cilantro

METHOD

■ This recipe is cooked in two operations—roasting the duckling, which takes 30 minutes per pound, or a total of 2 hours for a 4-pound duckling, and cooking the sweet and sour sauce, which takes about 30 minutes.

METHOD

■ Preheat the oven to 425°F. Make sure that the cavity of the duckling is empty, and then place the duckling in a roasting pan and roast for 20 minutes.

■ Reduce the oven temperature to 350°F. Remove the duckling and baste, pouring off the excess fat, then return it to the oven and bake for another 20 minutes. Repeat this process 3 more times over the next hour.

■ Meanwhile, make the sauce. Heat the duck fat in a frying pan and sauté the garlic and onion for 5 minutes. Add the cumin, turmeric, and cinnamon and sauté for another 2 or 3 minutes. Let the mixture cool, and then purée in a blender or food processor, adding enough water to achieve a creamy texture. Return the mixture to the frying pan, and add the almonds and enough water to create a thick sauce.

■ The distinctive taste of this dish is the sweet and sour achieved traditionally by using pomegranate (sour) and molasses (sweet). In a separate small pan, boil the water and add the pomegranate seeds to it. Simmer for 5 minutes, cool, then push the flesh through a strainer. Return the liquid to the pan. Add the sugar, and lemon juice if you want a tarter taste. Add this to the sauce. You should now have about 2 1/2 cups of thick, rich sauce.

■ Remove the duckling from the oven after 1 hour and drain off all the fat. Baste the duckling with one-third of the sauce. Return it to the oven and bake for a final 20 to 30 minutes, or until tender, basting it twice more, and using all the sauce.

■ To serve, center the duckling on a large oval platter and pour all the reserved sauce over it. Garnish with pomegranate seeds or red currants, pistachio nuts, and cilantro. Serve with rice.

FISH AND SEAFOOD DISHES

▲▲▲▲▲▲▲▲▲▲▲▲▲▲▲▲▲

The Middle East encompasses a vast amount of coastline which encloses many seas including the Mediterranean, Black, Red, Caspian, and Arabian seas, and the Persian Gulf. Three great rivers, the Nile, the Tigris, and the Euphrates, have dominated the development of civilized man, and there are a number of natural lakes and man-made dams throughout the whole area. Fishing was well-established by the ancient hunter-gatherer tribes, long before man learned about agriculture. Fish were being farmed in pens in natural lakes by the ancient Egyptians, and many examples of fish preserved by smoking and drying have been discovered in the Pyramids.

The warm waters of the Middle East contain thousands of species of fish, of which about 150 are regularly consumed, and hundreds of species of crustaceans and mollusks. Many of these are now available fresh and frozen at good markets. My selection of recipes features a large variety of fish including swordfish, mullet, mackerel, sardines, anchovy, cod, haddock, trout, salmon, sea trout, and monkfish, and of seafood including shrimp, king prawns, lobster, and crawfish. You can widen this selection yourself by using the fish or seafood of your preference. The cooking methods in this chapter are equally varied and include grilling, barbecuing, casseroling, baking, currying, stewing, frying, grinding, and stuffing.

Fish is now recognized as being one of the healthiest foods we can eat because it is high in protein and low in fat.

Skewered Swordfish

KILICH SHISH

SERVES 4

Walk past any seaside cafe in Turkey and you will be tantalized by the aroma of fish sizzling over charcoal. Fat, skewered cubes of fish drip their oily herbal marinade onto the coals and in a few minutes they are served inside pita bread for a snack, or with rice and a garlic and lemon dip for a more substantial meal.

Use a large fish with firm white flesh. Swordfish is traditional, fresh or frozen. Alternatives include shark, barracuda, or halibut.

INGREDIENTS

2 pounds swordfish	1/2 teaspoon aromatic salt (see page 23)
6 tablespoons olive oil	6 tablespoons hazelnut oil
2 tablespoons lemon juice	2 tablespoons lemon juice
1/4 cup minced onion	2 tablespoons minced cilantro
2 teaspoons paprika	2 to 6 cloves garlic, minced
1 teaspoon ground white pepper	1 teaspoon coarsely ground black pepper
1/2 teaspoon ground bay leaf	1/2 teaspoon aromatic salt (see page 23)

METHOD

■ Remove the skin and cut the fish into large pieces about 1 1/2 inches in length, which should yield approximately 24 cubes. (Save the trimmings for fish soup or stock.)

■ To make the marinade, in a bowl whisk together the olive oil, lemon juice, onion, paprika, pepper, bay leaf, and salt. Add the fish cubes and marinate in the refrigerator for up to 2 hours.

■ Preheat the broiler to medium, and place the rack on the lowest level. Thread the fish onto 4 skewers, making sure that the cubes are well coated with marinade.

■ Broil for 10 minutes, turning once or twice. Or you can grill over charcoal.

■ Meanwhile, to make the dipping sauce, mix together the hazelnut oil, lemon juice, cilantro, garlic, pepper, and salt in a bowl.

■ Serve by removing the grilled fish from the skewers and arrange on a plate with the cold dip.

Mullet Casserole

BALIKLAR PLAKI

SERVES 4

This style of cooking originated in the Byzantine era centuries ago, and is still widely used in Greece, Turkey, and Armenia. Fish or vegetables are baked in olive oil with garlic, herbs, and tomato. Traditionally the fish would simply be chopped up and added to the other ingredients, head, tail, skin, bones, and all, and fish devotees may prefer this method. Personally, I prefer to skin and fillet the fish first. Mullet, grey or red, is often used for this dish, but any fish is equally suitable. A favorite Armenian version of this dish uses mackerel and is called uskumru plaki.

INGREDIENTS

1 1/2 pounds grey or red mullet	3 or 4 sticks celery, diced into 1/2-inch pieces
6 tablespoons olive oil	6 canned plum tomatoes, chopped
2 teaspoons paprika	4 to 8 cloves garlic
1 cup onion, cut into rings	4 bay leaves
1 cup fish stock or water	salt and pepper to taste
1/2 cup carrot, thinly sliced	

METHOD

■ Remove the skin and bones and cut the fish into pieces about 2 1/2 inches square.

■ In a skillet or wok, heat the oil and sauté the paprika and onion for 5 minutes. Add the fish stock or water, simmer, then add the carrot, celery, tomatoes, garlic, and bay leaves.

■ Continue to simmer for about 20 minutes, allowing the liquid to reduce by one-third. Season with salt and pepper.

■ Preheat the oven to 375°F. Place the cooking liquid into a large casserole dish, then add the fish. Bake, uncovered, for 20 minutes. Test for tenderness—it will probably require about 10 more minutes. Add a little water, if necessary.

Pan-Fried Sardines

SARDALYA TAVASI

SERVES 4

The simplest things are often the best and fried sardines are one of those things. Found in all Middle Eastern coastal towns, they sizzle away on racks over charcoal or in frying pans. This Turkish recipe uses a shallow griddle pan, or tava, and makes a great appetizer or mezzeh dish. Choose sardines of about 2 ounces each and about 4 inches long, and serve two per person for an appetizer. If the fish are smaller, allow about 4 ounces per person. This recipe is also ideal for tiny fish such as sprats, whitebait, and anchovy.

INGREDIENTS

8 2-ounce whole sardines	salt to taste
sunflower oil for frying	lemon slices
all-purpose flour	

METHOD

- Wash the fish and pat dry with paper towels.

- Heat the oil in a large frying pan.

- Roll the fish in the flour and place it in the pan. Fry it for about 10 minutes, turning it over and adding oil as necessary.

- Remove and set aside in a warm oven while you cook the remaining fish.

- Sprinkle with salt and serve with a twist of lemon.

Spicy Fried Shrimps

NACHBOUS

SERVES 4

The seafood from the Persian Gulf is of outstanding quality, as are the recipes for cooking it. Nachbous is a particularly delicious fried shrimp recipe which is found in Kuwait, Bahrain, and Saudi Arabia. It uses curry spices and is usually cooked slowly with rice; in this version, the shrimps are cooked separately and served with the rice.

INGREDIENTS

2 pounds shrimp or prawns	6 tablespoons clarified butter or vegetable oil
1 teaspoon baharat (see page 19)	4 to 8 cloves garlic, minced
1/2 teaspoon turmeric	1 cup minced onion
1 teaspoon ground cumin	2 tablespoons minced cilantro
1 teaspoon mild curry powder	aromatic salt to taste (see page 23)
1 to 2 teaspoons cayenne or to taste	

METHOD

■ Remove the shells, devein, and wash the shrimps. If frozen, thaw them in a strainer.

■ In a bowl, combine the baharat, turmeric, cumin, curry powder, and cayenne with enough water to make a paste of pouring consistency. Set aside.

■ In a wok or deep-frying pan, heat the clarified butter or oil and sauté the garlic for 1 minute, then add the spice paste and sauté for 2 or 3 minutes. Add the onion and continue to cook for about 10 more minutes.

■ Add the shrimp and cilantro and simmer for 15 minutes. Add a little water if the shrimp becomes too dry. Stir occasionally and season with salt and pepper.

■ Serve with rice and khoubiz bread.

Fish Balls

GEFILTE

SERVES 4

Wherever there is a Jewish community, there is sure to be gefilte. They are small balls of ground fish, deep-fried or boiled, and served as a main-course meal with rice and vegetables or as a hot or cold appetizer. There are a number of recipes for gefilte in Israel. This one is typical.

INGREDIENTS

1 1/2 pounds white fish	1/4 cup breadcrumbs
1/2 cup chopped onion	salt and pepper to taste
2 eggs	vegetable oil for deep-frying

METHOD

■ Remove the skin and bones and cut the fish into pieces suitable for grinding.

■ Place all the ingredients in a blender or food processor and blend to achieve a sticky paste texture.

■ Divide the mixture into 4 portions, then subdivide each quarter into 4, 6, or 8 balls, depending on the size you desire.

■ Heat the oil in a deep-fryer to 375°F. One by one, place the balls into the oil, until half of them are in the fryer, and cook for 7 or 8 minutes. Remove from the pan, drain on paper towels, and keep them warm while you fry the second batch. Serve cold as a snack or hot with French fries and a twist of lemon.

The following are two variations of this recipe. The Turkish version, baliklar koftesi, can be made by following the preceding recipe and adding 1 teaspoon paprika, 1/2 teaspoon ground cumin, and 1/2 teaspoon ground allspice. The Arab version, blehat samak, can be made from the Turkish version with the addition of 1 teaspoon garlic powder and 1 teaspoon chopped cilantro. Shape them into fish fingers and cook according to the recipe instructions.

Fish Couscous

KESKSHEH BIL HOUT

SERVES 4

This is usually cooked by putting the entire fish into the bottom part of a couscous double steamer. This produces a tasty but rather bony, scaly, mushy mixture, much adored by those accustomed to it. I prefer this Libyan method where fish fillets are used. To cook the couscous see page 133. (You can, of course, serve the fish with rice as an alternative.)

INGREDIENTS

1 1/2 pounds white fish	4 canned tomatoes, chopped
1 cup smoked haddock, cut into small pieces, complete with the skin	2 teaspoons whole black peppercorns
	1 teaspoon ground cumin
3 cups water	1 teaspoon bahar (see page 19)
4 bay leaves	2 tablespoons clarified butter
1 cup chopped onion	20 saffron threads
4 cloves garlic	1 tablespoon chopped cilantro
2 carrots, diced	salt to taste
2 sticks celery, diced	1 recipe couscous (page 133)

METHOD

■ Remove the skin, heads, tails, and bones from the fish and reserve. Cut the fish into large chunks and set aside.

■ Bring the water to a boil and add the fish heads, tails, skin, and bones along with the haddock and bay leaves. Reduce the heat and simmer for 1 hour. Strain. Discard the solids and return the liquid to the pan and return to a simmer.

■ Add the onion, garlic, carrots, celery, tomatoes, peppercorns, cumin, bahar, and the clarified butter. Simmer for 30 to 40 minutes.

■ Add the chunks of fish and continue to simmer for about 10 more minutes.

■ Add the saffron and cilantro and season with salt. Simmer for 5 more minutes and serve piping hot with couscous.

Spicy Marinated Grilled Trout

CHERMOULA SAMAK

SERVES 4

Chermoula is a spicy coating or marinating paste from Morocco. It is widely used with meat dishes. In this recipe the paste is rubbed into fish steaks and the fish is left to marinate before broiling. Sea bass or bream are normally used, but freshwater trout is a delicious alternative.

INGREDIENTS

4 12-ounce trout	1 recipe chermoula (see page 19)

METHOD

- Clean and gut the trout, keeping them in one piece, then carefully wash and dry them..

- Cut each trout into 4 pieces and immerse them in the chermoula marinade in a large, nonmetal bowl.

- Cover the bowl and refrigerate at least 6 hours (a maximum of 24 hours).

- Preheat the broiler to medium hot. Place the rack at its lowest level.

- Place the fish pieces on a wire rack and broil for 10 to 15 minutes, turning twice. Serve with rice.

Baked Lobster

ISTAKOZ FIRINDA

SERVES 4

Lobster is a luxury everywhere, but this subtle Turkish recipe does more than justice to the succulent creatures that are readily available in the Istanbul fish market.

INGREDIENTS

4 1-pound lobsters	1 teaspoon minced dill
3 tablespoons vegetable oil	2/3 cup sour cream or cream cheese
2 cloves garlic, minced	1 teaspoon corn flour
1/2 cup minced onion	salt to taste
1 teaspoon paprika	chopped cilantro
1 tablespoon minced parsley	

METHOD

■ In a large stockpot, boil fresh lobsters for 15 minutes, then remove and set aside to cool. If frozen, allow to thaw completely. Cut the shells in two and remove all the flesh. Discard the long black vein running from tail to head and the stomach sac which is in the head. The remaining flesh, including that in the claws, the bluish liver and any roe, is edible. Chop the meat into bite-size pieces. Set aside the shells for presentation.

■ In a large skillet or wok, heat the oil and sauté the garlic and onion for 3 minutes. Add the paprika, parsley, dill, sour cream or cream cheese, and corn flour, and stir briskly, adding a little water until it stops thickening. Season with salt, then add the lobster meat, stirring for 2 or 3 minutes.

■ Preheat the oven to 325°F. Carefully fill the lobster shells with the meat mixture, and place them on two baking sheets. Bake for 10 to 15 minutes.

■ Garnish with cilantro, and serve with rice.

Cod Baked with Tahini

SAMAK BIL TAHINI

SERVES 4

This classic Lebanese fish dish is baked in the sesame seed paste, tahini. Traditionally and deliciously, it is served with tabouli salad and taratoor b'snorbeh, a pine nut dip. You can use any fish of your choice, with or without heads, skin and bone, but I prefer to use cod fillet steak which gives the chunky texture that the dish requires.

INGREDIENTS

1 1/2 pounds cod fillet steak	1 cup milk
3 tablespoons olive oil	2 tablespoons tahini (see page 20)
2 to 4 cloves garlic, minced	aromatic salt to taste (see page 23)
1/2 cup minced onion	lemon wedges
1 tablespoon dried mint	1 tablespoon minced cilantro

METHOD

- Remove the skin and bones and cut the fish into 1 1/2-inch cubes.

- In a large skillet or wok, heat the oil and sauté the garlic and onion for 10 minutes. Add the mint, milk, and tahini and combine thoroughly.

- Preheat the oven to 375°F. Place the fish on a baking sheet.

- Coat the fish with the fried mixture, season with salt, and bake for about 20 minutes.

- Garnish with lemon wedges and cilantro.

Baked Curried Salmon or Sea Trout

MASGOUF BAGHDADI

SERVES 4

The recipe comes from a very luxurious hotel—the Regency—in Kuwait, whose 60-chef kitchen is renowned throughout the region. However, it seems that this dish is actually from Iraq. The fish they use is a freshwater fish called shabbat, which is a kind of salmon or trout.

INGREDIENTS

1 whole 3-pound sea trout or 1 2-pound piece of salmon	6 to 8 cloves garlic
2 teaspoons cumin	1 1-inch piece ginger
1 teaspoon baharat (see page 19)	1 onion, sliced
1 teaspoon cinnamon	6 tablespoons clarified butter or vegetable oil
I teaspoon coriander	6 canned plum tomatoes, chopped
1 teaspoon black mustard seed	aromatic salt to taste (see page 23)
1/2 teaspoon caraway	olive oil for final basting
1/2 teaspoon green cardamom	lemon wedges
1/2 teaspoon fenugreek seed	fresh fennel and cilantro

METHOD

■ Wash the fish, dry with paper towels, and cut small diagonal slashes in the flesh to allow the coating to penetrate.

■ To make the spice paste, in a bowl combine the cumin, baharat, cinnamon, coriander, mustard seed, caraway, cardamom, and fenugreek seed with enough water to make a paste of pouring consistency. Set aside to blend.

■ Place the garlic, ginger, and onion into a blender or food processor and purée.

■ In a skillet or wok, heat the clarified butter or oil and sauté the purée for 10 minutes. Add the spice paste and continue to cook for another 5 minutes. Add the tomatoes, and season with salt.

■ Preheat the oven to 275°F. Line one or two baking sheets with aluminum foil to prevent the fish from sticking. Arrange the fish on the trays, and cover with the fried mixture, working it into the fish. Cover the fish with foil, and bake for 1 1/2 hours.

METHOD

- Preheat the broiler. Remove the fish from the oven, and discard the top foil. The fish should be cooked and fairly dry. Baste it with a little olive oil, then place under the broiler for 2 or 3 minutes until it becomes crisp.

- Garnish with lemon wedges, fennel, and cilantro. Serve with rice.

Stuffed Monkfish

MAHI NOW ROOZ

SERVES 4

There is a thriving fishing industry in Iran, and a corresponding selection of fish recipes to match. On one traditional occasion each year, fish is eaten throughout Iran. At the New Year (Now Rooz), celebrated on the 21st of March, which is the first day of spring, fish is traditionally eaten throughout the country.

This stuffed fish recipe is delicious at any time of year. It calls for any plump, firm fish, but my personal preference is monkfish. This fish is so ugly, with its vast red-lipped, spiky-toothed mouth, that it is almost always sold headless and skinned. But its flesh is amazingly tasty, resembling that of lobster or king prawns, and is ideal for stuffing, having a deep, round pocket if carefully boned.

INGREDIENTS

1 1- to 1 1/2-pound monkfish tail	1 tablespoon chopped almonds
1 pound fresh spinach, washed and finely shredded	1 tablespoon chopped walnuts
	1 tablespoon chopped pistachio nuts
4 tablespoons clarified butter or vegetable oil	1/2 teaspoon aromatic salt (see page 23)
	1/2 cup yogurt
1/2 cup minced onion	2 tablespoons ketchup
2 tablespoons brown sugar	2 to 4 cloves garlic, minced
1 tablespoon sultanas	1 teaspoon turmeric
8 dates, seeded and chopped	1 teaspoon powdered cinnamon
6 cherry tomatoes, quartered	2 tablespoons walnut oil
1 loumi (dried lime), quartered	fresh or dried mint
1 teaspoon zereshk (dried barberries)	lime wedges

METHOD

- Carefully bone the fish, leaving a pouch to hold the stuffing, then wash and pat it dry. Set aside.

- To start the stuffing, blanch the spinach for 2 minutes, strain, and set aside.

- Meanwhile, prepare the coating. In a bowl, whisk the yogurt, ketchup, garlic, turmeric, cinnamon, and walnut oil together with a fork. Set aside.

- In a skillet or wok, heat the clarified butter or oil and sauté the onion for about 5 minutes. Add the sugar and when it has melted, add the sultanas, dates, tomatoes, loumi, zereshk, the nuts, salt, and the spinach. Reduce the heat and simmer for a few minutes, stirring to blend and soften the mixture. Set aside to cool.

- Preheat the oven to 375°F. Spread aluminum foil on a baking sheet to prevent the fish from sticking. Carefully stuff the fish—don't overstuff. Try to enclose the stuffing, and set aside any extra.

- Place the fish on the baking sheet and baste it with one-third of the coating mixture.

- Bake for 20 minutes. Turn the fish over, baste with another third of the coating mixture, and bake for another 20 minutes.

- Then turn it again and baste with the remaining coating mixture and bake for 10 to 20 more minutes.

- Garnish with mint and lime wedges.

VEGETABLE AND EGG DISHES

▲▲▲▲▲▲▲▲▲▲▲▲▲▲▲▲▲▲

As we have seen, Middle Eastern cooking has roots that go back to the earliest human civilizations. Always at hand are a very wide selection of vegetables that grow indigenously, and cultivation inspired interesting manners of preparation. These vegetables included eggplant, beet, fava beans, cabbage, carrots, cauliflower, zucchini, cucumber, garlic, globe artichokes, grapevine leaves, leeks, lettuce, squash, mushrooms, okra, olives, onions, peas, spinach, and turnips.

The early farmers soon learned that the seeds of plants of the legume family were edible and could be eaten fresh, but more importantly, they could be dried. This discovery enabled beans, lentils, and chickpeas to be stored against winters and famines. These ingredients have also provided a wealth of nutritious and delicious dishes, and are still the backbone of today's Middle Eastern cuisine. I have included several such ancient and traditional recipes in this chapter. But you may notice that many familiar vegetables are missing from these dishes such as avocados, bell peppers, chile peppers, string beans, Jerusalem artichokes, corn, plantains, potatoes, tomatoes, and celery. All of these were discovered in the New World in the sixteenth century (along with chocolate, peanuts, tobacco, turkeys, and vanilla). When these "new" vegetables soon arrived in the Old World, they were adopted and cultivated and are now an inextricable part of Middle Eastern cooking.

Also in this chapter are recipes for egg dishes, the celebrated stuffed vine-leaf dish, dolmas, and an intriguing noodle dish. I should mention finally that it is very common for meat to be cooked with vegetable dishes in Middle Eastern cooking. However, all the recipes in this chapter are meat-free.

Green Vegetables

MELOKHIA

SERVES 4

Melokhia is a green leafy vegetable that has been grown in Egypt for thousands of years. It is a little like spinach in color and texture, with oval leaves growing on long stalks, but it is considerably smaller, the average leaf being about 3 inches. As it is difficult, if not impossible, to obtain in the West, spinach may be used instead.

The *melokhia* is normally chopped very finely with a *makhrata*, a sharp crescent-shaped, two-handled blade (identical to the *mezzaluna* used in Europe) by rotating it over the vegetables. The other method is harder but more elegant, and requires the leaves to be "shaved" into long, very thin strips, like Chinese seaweed. A cleaver may be used to achieve this.

INGREDIENTS

2 3/4 pounds fresh spinach	6 to 8 green cardamoms
2 cups water or chicken stock	2 to 4 teaspoons ground coriander
4 to 8 cloves garlic, minced	6 canned tomatoes (optional)
1 cup chopped onion	ta'leyah to taste (see page 40)
6 to 8 bay leaves	

METHOD

■ Wash and dry the spinach, discarding the stalks, and chop as described above.

■ In a stockpot, bring the water or stock to a boil, and add all the ingredients except the spinach and *ta'leyah*. Reduce the heat and simmer for 1 hour.

■ Blanch the leaves in a separate pan of boiling water for a couple of minutes. Strain and add to the simmering stockpot. Mix well and serve as soon as the leaves are cooked to your liking.

■ Garnish with the *ta'leyah*.

Shredded Potato Cakes

LATKES

SERVES 4 (12 LATKES)

These are delicious fried patties, enjoyed by Jewish communities the world over, at all times of the year, but particularly to celebrate Jewish religious festivals. I will never forget the first encounter I had with latkes. I was in a New York yellow cab whose driver was a little, fat, talkative fellow from the Bronx. I was intending to travel downtown from 54th Street for about twenty blocks, which should have taken about 10 minutes. When he realized I was English he decided to tell me about New York, with the nonstop patter of virtually all taxi drivers, while stuffing his face with something golden in color. Suddenly he offered me one. "Mama" (his wife) had cooked it the day before, he said, advising me that it was a latke. I asked him where in New York I could get them. The upshot was that he turned the meter off, after ensuring that I had time to spare, and whisked me off to a taxi drivers' Jewish café on Orchard Street near the Manhattan Bridge. The street outside was crowded with illegally parked yellow cabs and police cars, and the café was packed with their drivers. I got my latkes and spent a most enjoyable hour.

INGREDIENTS

1 pound potatoes	1/2 teaspoon ground white pepper
1 cup minced onion	1/2 teaspoon salt
1 egg	1 teaspoon white sugar
1 tablespoon corn flour	vegetable oil for frying
3/4 cup all-purpose flour	

METHOD

■ Scrub and peel the potatoes, then cut into julienne or grate (by hand or by machine, pulsing carefully or else it goes mushy). Rinse in cold water to remove the starch.

■ Mix all the ingredients together except the oil in a bowl, adding just enough water to form a stiff paste.

■ Divide the mixture into 12 equal portions, then press each one into an oval shape about 3 1/2 inches long. In a large frying pan, heat the oil and fry the patties 4 at a time, turning 2 or 3 times until golden brown. Serve with pastrami and bagels.

Zucchini Stuffed with Kibbeh

KOSSA MASHIYA BIL KIBBEH

SERVES 4

Zucchini looks especially attractive when stuffed, and this Lebanese recipe uses a kibbeh mixture (see page 68) as a stuffing, For a nonmeat alternative, try bulgur. The success of the dish depends on using small zucchini, and on coring them neatly. Use a very slim sharp knife to cut with and a wooden spoon handle with which to push out the filling.

INGREDIENTS

16 zucchini, each about 3 inches long	1/2 recipe kibbeh (see page 68)
4 tablespoons vegetable oil	1 teaspoon baharat (see page 19)
1/4 cup minced onion	

METHOD

■ Wash the zucchini and trim the tops and tails. Carefully remove the center core (retaining it for future use), as described above. Leave about 1/4 inch of skin and flesh all round, and don't pierce the skin or it will split during cooking.

■ In a skillet or wok, heat the oil and sauté the onion, *kibbeh* or bulgur, and *baharat* for 7 or 8 minutes. Strain and let cool. Preheat the oven to 325°F.

■ Carefully stuff the zucchini with the cooled mixture and line them up side by side in a baking dish.

■ Bake for 15 minutes.

Zucchini Fritters

KABAK MUCVER

SERVES 4
(8 FRITTERS)

I have included this Turkish recipe because it solves the problem of what to do with the cores of the zucchini from the previous recipe. The answer is to freeze them until you decide to make this recipe.

INGREDIENTS

4 tablespoons corn flour	1 cup chopped onion
4 tablespoons all-purpose flour	2 cloves garlic, minced
aromatic salt (see page 23) and pepper to taste	1/2 cup grated cheddar or feta cheese
2 eggs	2 tablespoons chopped cilantro
16 zucchini cores, mashed	1/2 cup plus 1 tablespoon vegetable oil

METHOD

■ Mix the flours in a bowl and add just enough water to make a thick paste. Season with salt and pepper and beat in the eggs.

■ Add all the remaining ingredients except for the oil.

■ Heat the oil in a large flat frying pan. With a large spoon, scoop out about an eighth of the mixture, and drop it into the pan. Press it down with the back of the spoon to create a thick disc shape. Repeat with 3 more.

■ Fry these 4 discs about 8 to 10 minutes, turning once or twice, until golden.

■ Repeat with the remainder of the mixture. Serve hot as an appetizer or side dish.

Jerusalem Artichoke in Olive Oil

YERELMASI ZEYTINYAGLI

SERVES 4

The Jerusalem artichoke is a tuber with a sweet and nutty flavor. Originally from North America, it is not related to globe artichokes, being a species of sunflower, and by the way has nothing to do with Jerusalem either, having gained its name from the Italian word for sunflower, *girasole*. This Turkish recipe simmers the artichoke with carrots, celery, and rice.

INGREDIENTS

3/4 pound Jerusalem artichokes	3 tablespoons dry basmati rice
4 tablespoons olive oil	3/4 cup vegetable stock or water
1/2 cup chopped onion	salt to taste
1/2 cup carrots, peeled and thinly sliced	1 lemon
1/2 cup celery, chopped	chopped parsley

METHOD

■ Pare the artichokes and remove knobbles and scars in much the same way as for ginger. Immediately cut into 1/2-inch cubes, and keep in cold water to prevent discoloring.

■ In a skillet or wok, heat the oil and sauté the onion for 5 minutes. Strain the artichokes and add them to the onion, with the carrots, celery, and rice. Cook for about 5 minutes, then add the stock or water and bring to a boil. Reduce the heat and simmer for about 20 minutes. Add more water, if necessary.

■ Season with salt and serve with a squeeze of lemon and a sprinkling of parsley.

Globe Artichoke

ENGINAR ZEYTINYAGLI

SERVES 4

This recipe uses the other artichoke, the globe artichoke, which is a variety of thistle and is indigenous to North Africa. Indeed artichokes are very cheap and plentiful there and appear in salads and tagines.

INGREDIENTS

4 globe artichokes	1/2 cup carrots, thinly sliced
2 tablespoons vinegar	1 tablespoon sugar
2 tablespoons olive oil	1 teaspoon salt
16 tiny whole pickling onions	1 teaspoon black pepper
1 teaspoon powdered cinnamon	1 lemon
1/2 cup fava beans, fresh or frozen and thawed	chopped parsley

METHOD

■ Wash the artichokes to remove grit. Heat 8 cups of water in a stockpot and boil the artichokes in the water for 15 minutes. Remove and set aside to cool.

■ Cut away the leaves and expose the base. Cut away the top half. Scoop out the hairy filaments of the choke. Remove the stem from the base and then trim the hard outer parts from the base and sides. Place the prepared hearts into a bowl of cold water with the vinegar to prevent discoloration.

■ In a large saucepan, heat the oil and sauté the onions, cinnamon, fava beans, and carrots for 10 minutes. Add the artichokes and water to cover, reduce the heat, and simmer for about 1 hour. Add more water, if necessary.

■ Just before serving, add the sugar, salt, and pepper. Garnish with a squeeze of lemon and sprinkling of parsley.

■ **N**ote: Use the leaves to start a vegetable stock. Simmer for 1 hour, then strain and discard them.

Stir-Fried Okra

BAMIYA B'ZAYT

SERVES 4 AS
AN ENTRÉE

Okra is the pod of a plant native to Africa. Okra has always been an important vegetable in Middle Eastern cuisine. The traditional way of cooking okra, or *bamiya*, is to stew it for half an hour or so until it is sappy and sticky. Personally, I find this texture not to my taste, and prefer a more crunchy okra. This Lebanese method uses a quick, stir-fry technique which retains all the delicate flavors and texture.

INGREDIENTS

8 tablespoons olive oil, divided	1 tablespoon lemon juice
4 to 8 cloves garlic, minced	1 tablespoon sugar
1 tablespoon ground coriander	1 tablespoon chopped cilantro
1 cup chopped onion	aromatic salt (see page 23) and black pepper to taste
1 14-ounce can plum tomatoes and juice	
1 1/2 pounds tender fresh okra	

METHOD

■ In a wok or large frying pan, heat half the oil and sauté the garlic for 1 minute, then add the coriander and sauté another minute. Add the onion and cook for 5 minutes.

■ Add the tomatoes and their juice, reduce the heat, and simmer, stirring occasionally.

■ Meanwhile, wash and dry the okra and cut off the pointed tip and the stalk and discard them.

■ Transfer the contents of the wok into a large mixing bowl.

■ Heat the remaining oil in the wok, and while it is heating, cut the okra into 1-inch pieces. Place them immediately into the wok and gently toss for 5 minutes.

■ Add the reserved tomato mixture plus the lemon juice, sugar, and cilantro. Continue to simmer and season with salt and pepper. Serve at once. (Do not store or freeze this dish as it will go mushy.)

Sautéed Celery

KEREVIZ TEREYAGLI

SERVES 4

This is one of the simplest vegetable dishes, coming from Turkey as do so many delicious recipes.

INGREDIENTS

1 1/2 pounds celery	aromatic salt to taste (see page 23)
1/3 cup clarified butter or butter	1 tablespoon lemon juice
1 tablespoon za'atar (see page 20) (optional)	

METHOD

- Wash the celery, and discard the thin stalks and leaves, which are usually bitter. Chop into 2-inch chunks.

- Blanch the celery in boiling water for 3 to 5 minutes, then strain (reserve the water for future stock).

- Heat the clarified butter or butter in a wok. Add the hot celery and sauté for 3 or 4 minutes. Add the remaining ingredients and cook for another few minutes. Serve hot.

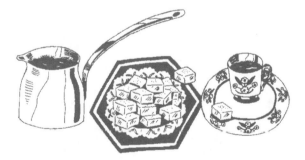

Sautéed Leeks

BRAS YAHNI

SERVES 4

From Armenia comes this light leek dish, with a hint of sweetness which, if you wish, can be made more pronounced by adding more sugar. The Saudi version of this dish is called *korrat bi zayt* and it uses a miniature type of leek called *korrat*. Use scallions in combination with leeks for this version and omit the sugar.

INGREDIENTS

1 pound leeks	1 bunch watercress, chopped
4 tablespoons vegetable or olive oil	1 bunch scallions (optional)
2 to 6 cloves garlic	1 to 3 teaspoons cayenne (optional)
4 fresh tomatoes, chopped	salt to taste
1 to 3 tablespoons brown sugar (optional)	1 cup yahni stock (see page 27) or water

METHOD

■ Wash the leeks carefully, as mud often remains between the leaves. Shake dry, then cut off the hairy root ends and any spoiled leaf tips or leaves. Chop into pieces about 1 1/2 inches in length.

■ In a large skillet or wok, heat the oil and sauté the garlic for 1 minute, then add all the remaining and optional items except the stock and leeks, cooking for another 3 minutes.

■ Add the leeks and when sizzling, pour in the stock or water. Reduce the heat and simmer for 10 to 15 minutes, stirring occasionally, to desired tenderness.

Ratatouille-Style Vegetables

CHAKCHOUKA

SERVES 4

The *chakchouka* or *tchoutchouka* is a style of vegetable cooking from the Maghreb. It generally contains garlic and onion fried in olive oil with tomatoes, peppers, and a principal vegetable such as zucchini, squash, eggplant, artichoke, cauliflower, beans, etc., and resembles the Turkish *plaki* or the French *ratatouille*. Very often *chakchouka* dishes are finished by pouring beaten eggs over the dish at the final stages of cooking.

INGREDIENTS

3 tablespoons sunflower oil	2 to 6 fresh green or red chiles, chopped (optional)
2 cloves garlic, minced	1 teaspoon cumin seeds (optional)
1 cup chopped onion	2 teaspoons brown sugar
1 red and/or green bell pepper, stemmed, , seeded, and chopped	salt to taste
1 14-ounce can tomatoes with juice	2 eggs (optional)
1 pound zucchini	1 tablespoon minced parsley
1 7-ounce can white haricot or fava beans with juice (optional)	

METHOD

■ In a wok or large frying pan, heat the oil and sauté the garlic for 1 minute. Then add the onion and cook for about 5 more minutes.

■ Add the peppers and the tomatoes with their juice. Reduce the heat and simmer for 10 minutes.

■ Meanwhile, prepare the zucchini. Wash and trim the zucchini and cut into 1-inch pieces. Blanch in boiling water for 3 minutes.

■ Strain (reserving water for future stock), and add to the wok along with the haricot or fava beans, if desired. Add the chiles and cumin, if desired, and sugar, and simmer for 5 minutes more. Season with salt.

■ For an Algerian version of this recipe, lightly beat the eggs with a fork, then pour them all over the *chakchouka*. Cook until the egg sets. Garnish with the parsley and serve hot with *khoubiz* bread or rice.

A Turkish *sebzeler plaki* can be made from the above recipe by omitting the spicy options and egg. And *chakchouka merguez* contains the Maghreb sausage, *merguez* (see page 50). Chop it up and add at the same time as the tomatoes and peppers.

119

White Haricot Beans

FASSOOLIA BAYDAH

SERVES 4

Fassoolia baydah is white dry haricot beans. As with many Middle Eastern vegetable dishes, more often than not, chunks of meat on the bone are simmered in the pot. This Syrian recipe omits the meat but it is still very tasty when served as a side dish with meat and bread or rice. Use either pearl haricots, the small white beans, or white haricots, the larger, creamy, flat beans.

INGREDIENTS

1 pound dry haricot beans	1/2 teaspoon freshly ground black pepper
4 tablespoons vegetable oil	6 tomatoes, chopped
2 to 4 cloves garlic, chopped	1 cup yahni stock (see page 27) or water
1 cup chopped onion	salt to taste
1/2 teaspoon ground green cardamom	lemon twists
1 teaspoon powdered cinnamon	chopped fresh herbs
1 teaspoon cayenne (optional)	

METHOD

■ Pick through the beans to ensure there is no grit, then rinse them in cold water a few times. Put them into a large bowl with plenty of cold water and leave them for between 12 and 24 hours.

■ On the following day, rinse the beans again. In a large stockpot, bring 8 cups of water to a boil, add the beans, and boil for at least an hour, until they are tender.

■ In a skillet or wok, heat the oil and sauté the garlic for 1 minute, then the onion for another 5 minutes. Add the cardamom, cinnamon, cayenne, if desired, and pepper and combine thoroughly. Then add the tomatoes and the stock or water, reduce the heat, and simmer for 5 to 10 minutes.

■ Add the drained beans and sauté for a few minutes. Serve hot, garnished with the lemon and herbs.

Brown Egyptian Beans

FUL MEDAMIS OR EL-FUL

SERVES 4 AS
AN ENTRÉE

This bean dish is described as Egypt's national dish, and it is astonishingly popular. The Egyptian word *ful* or *fool* means beans, and there are many types. Most popular are *ful roomi*, red kidney beans; *ful haman*, pigeon peas (or gunga peas or *toor dhal*); *ful baladi sa'idi*, white, middle-sized beans; *ful akdar*, green-skinned broad beans; *ful nabed*, brown-skinned broad beans; and *ful medamis*, small, round, brown broad beans with a small black stripe, also called tic, horse, or Egyptian brown beans. Confusion arises with the latter two types because they are both varieties of *fava* bean, and both are white when their brown skins are removed.

Ful cooking is taken very seriously in Egypt and a special cooking pot—the *damassa* or *idra*—is used just for the purpose. It is a vase-shaped metal pan with a narrow neck and tight-fitting lid. It holds a small amount of water and the neck design causes the water to condense and drop back into the pan so that the water will last throughout the cooking time. The two recipes that follow are from the Falfela restaurant, Hoda Sharawi Street, Cairo; it's very inexpensive and is always full of local people enjoying good local food. One section of their menu has 15 different *ful* dishes ranging from *ful* with oil to *ful* with *pastruma* and eggs.

INGREDIENTS

1 1/4 cup ful medamis	1 teaspoon aromatic salt (see page 23)
1 recipe ta'leyah (see page 40)	2 tablespoons olive oil
1 teaspoon ground cumin	lemon wedges, for garnish
2 tablespoons minced parsley	

METHOD

■ Pick through the dry beans, removing grit or withered ones. Rinse, then soak them in a bowl large enough to accommodate the beans as they swell, with 3 times their volume of cold water. Refrigerate for 24 hours.

■ On the following day, rinse the beans. Bring 1 1/2 times their volume of water to a boil in a stockpot and add the beans. Reduce the heat and simmer until the beans are tender but not mushy. Test for tenderness after 1 hour (cooking times vary depending on the type of bean). It is more likely to take 2 or even 3 hours. Add more water if needed, but be careful not to add too much. The finished dish should have whole beans in a little creamy liquid.

■ Add the remaining ingredients and combine thoroughly. Garnish with lemon wedges, and serve hot with *aiysh* (see page 147), salads, and yogurt.

121

Egyptian Fava Beans

FUL NABED

The same recipe is used to cook these larger beans. After the soaking period squeeze off the brown skins to reveal bright white beans. Follow the instructions for the recipe. They should cook quicker than *ful medamis*. This dish can be served as in the previous recipe. Alternatively, both recipes can be served as soup by puréeing the beans and adding water to the desired consistency.

Brown Lentils

'ADS BI GIBBA

SERVES 4

The Arabic word for lentils is *'ads* (*adas* in Iran). The most popular lentils in the Gulf and the Levant are yellow split lentils (*'ads asfar*), which are used in soups and stews, and brown whole lentils with skins (*'ads bi gibba*, literally lentils in a cloak). These local brown lentils are small, hard, round pellets, which require long soaking and cooking time, but which retain their shape and are good for soups and sautées as well as stews. A good substitute is the French *puy* lentil.

The imported Indian brown lentil (*masoor dhal*) can also be used. Called *'ads iswid*, they are the familiar red (orange) lentils, which have pale brown skins. They tend to go very soft when cooked.

This recipe is from Jordan. A virtually identical Egyptian variation omits the celery but calls for 20 cloves of garlic!

INGREDIENTS

1 cup whole brown lentils	1/2 cup celery, diced
1 recipe ta'leyah (see page 40)	aromatic salt to taste (see page 23)
1 teaspoon ground coriander	2 tablespoons olive oil (optional)
1 teaspoon cumin seeds	chopped fresh herbs

METHOD

▪ Pick through the lentils to remove any grit or debris, then soak them overnight in ample cold water in a large bowl.

▪ On the following day, rinse them several times, then put them into a stockpot with 1 1/2 times their volume of water and simmer until tender. (Timing will vary depending on lentil type, so test after 30 minutes, and then every 10 minutes after that.) Keep an eye on the water content. Add more if the lentils need it.

METHOD

■ While the lentils are cooking, make the ta'leyah.

■ If there is too much water remaining in the lentils, strain it off (keep for stock), then mix all the ingredients together back in the same stockpot and simmer for about 10 minutes. (Add in some lentil water, if necessary.)

■ Garnish with the olive oil, if desired, and herbs. Serve with rice and/or khoubiz bread for a complete and delicious meal.

Chickpeas with Spinach

HUMMUS YE ESFENAJ

SERVES 4

Chickpeas or hummus originated in the Middle East and are grown abundantly throughout the area, thriving in arid conditions. They can be used fresh, but they are most commonly bought dried, when they are milled into flour, coarsely ground for hummus (see page 32), or used whole as in this recipe. White chickpeas are used (there are also black or red varieties), and they must be soaked for 12 to 18 hours before cooking.
This combination of golden chickpeas interspersed with dark green strips of spinach is delightful in appearance as well as taste, and is found virtually unchanged in all the Middle Eastern countries.

INGREDIENTS

2 cups chickpeas	1 tablespoon brown sugar (Iranian and Armenian option)
3 tablespoons vegetable oil	2 teaspoons powdered cinnamon (Iranian and Turkish option)
2 to 4 cloves garlic, chopped	
1/2 cup chopped onion	4 to 6 canned tomatoes, plus juice
1 to 2 tablespoons harissa (see page 37) (Maghrebi option)	1 pound fresh spinach, finely sliced
1 tablespoon cumin seeds, roasted (Egyptian option)	aromatic salt (see page 23) and black pepper to taste
2 teaspoons baharat (see page 19) (Saudi option)	2 tablespoons clarified butter or olive oil
	1 tablespoon fresh lemon juice
	chopped fresh herbs

METHOD

■ Pick through the chickpeas for pieces of grit and debris. (Chickpeas are traditionally spread out on flat rooftops and dried in the sun which is why grit is commonly found in them.)

■ Rinse them, then soak in ample cold water in a large bowl. Let soak overnight, or for between 12 and 18 hours.

123

METHOD

■ Strain, rinse, then boil in a large stockpot of 10 cups boiling water. Reduce the heat and cook for 45 to 60 minutes, occasionally checking the water level.

■ Meanwhile, prepare the sauce and the spinach. In a large skillet or wok, heat the oil and sauté the garlic for 1 minute, then add the onion and sauté for 5 or 6 minutes. Add some or all of the options to your taste at this stage, and cook for 2 more minutes. Add the tomatoes and juice and lower the heat to a simmer.

■ In another stockpot, bring about 4 cups of water to a boil. Immerse the shredded spinach in it, reduce the heat, and simmer for 5 minutes. Strain and set aside.

■ As soon as the chickpeas are cooked until tender, strain them, discarding the water. Set aside to cool and freeze them (see note below) or, using the same stockpot, combine the sautéed mixture, spinach, and chickpeas, and return to a simmer. Season with salt and pepper.

■ Transfer to a serving bowl and garnish with curls of melted clarified butter or olive oil, lemon juice, and herbs. Serve with khoubiz bread or rice, salad, and pickles for a satisfying meal.

Lentils, Chickpeas, and Spinach

NOKHOD

A variation popular in the northern Levant and with the Kurdish peoples of western Iran uses a mixture of equal parts brown lentils and chickpeas, and is prepared in exactly the same way as the previous recipe.

French Fries with Spicy Sauce

BATATEH MA'LI BIL FELFEL SUDANI

SERVES 4

I have no idea whether this dish is authentic and where its place in history might be. I suspect it is modern, and the invention of the place where I ate it. But I don't think it really matters, as it is delicious, and as much a part of the Middle East as are any other recipes in this book. This one comes from Morocco; I encountered it, as they say in the movies, "on the road to Marrakesh." The city was up ahead, a lush festoon of green set in a dusty plain, framed by the high snowy peaks of the Atlas mountains behind it. The place was a nondescript roadside café. The meal on special was sausage and chips with red sauce. I was hungry, so I ordered it, never expecting a gastronomic experience. It just goes to show how wrong one can be. These chips were deep-fried in olive oil and saturated with fresh lemon juice. The sausage was merguez (see page 50) and the red sauce was homemade, hot, and spicy. *Felfel sudani* is the Moroccan version of harissa.

INGREDIENTS

1 to 1 1/2 pounds potatoes (quantity determined by the amount you want to eat)	merguez (see page 50) (optional)
	aromatic salt to taste (see page 23)
4 cups olive oil	juice of 2 lemons
1 recipe harissa (see page 37)	

METHOD

■ Wash, peel, and chop the potatoes to the length and thickness of your little finger. Leave them in cold water for 1 hour to reduce the starch content. Rinse and dry in paper towels.

■ Preheat the oil in a deep-fryer or saucepan to 375°F, then deep-fry half the potatoes for about 6 minutes, or until they are pale gold. Remove from the oil. Allow the oil temperature to return to 375°F and repeat with the remainder of the potatoes. Set aside.

■ Prepare the harissa, and heat it and the accompanying merguez, if desired.

■ Just before serving, return the oil to 375°F and refry for just a couple of minutes. Remove from the oil, and place on paper towels. Sprinkle with salt, drench with lemon juice, and serve at once.

Stuffed Vine Leaves

DOLMADES

**MAKES 24
DOLMADES**

All the countries of the Middle East have their dolma items, which can be traced back to before 1000 B.C., at the time of the Hittite Empire. The word *dolma* means "to stuff" (vegetables), and any suitable vegetable can be stuffed: artichokes, squash, zucchini, cabbage, and, more latterly, potatoes, tomatoes, and peppers. But by far the most popular "vegetable" for stuffing was and still is the grape vine leaf. Known as dolmades or *dolmathakia* in Greece, as *yaprakh dolmasi* in Turkey, *derevi sarma* or *dolma* in Armenia, *dolmeh-ye barge* in Iran, *wara-einab mishi* in the Levant, and *malfouf* in the Gulf, the stuffings can include rice, meat, fish, bulgur, or lentils.

The leaves themselves can occasionally be obtained fresh, but they are widely available packed in a brine in jars.

The dolmades are traditionally simmered on a stove in a heavy pan, and the water quantity is eventually absorbed. To prevent them from sticking and tearing when lifted out, the inside of the pan is lined with torn or excess vine leaves. The oven method is unconventional but easier.

INGREDIENTS

1 cup cooked and cooled rice	1 tablespoon ketchup
1 cup fried chopped onion	1 teaspoon bahar (see page 19)
1/2 cup pine nuts, roasted and chopped	1/2 teaspoon aromatic salt (see page 23)
1/4 cup chopped fresh mint	1 teaspoon white sugar
1/4 cup sultanas and/or dates, chopped (optional)	30 vine leaves (to allow for breakages)
	olive oil

METHOD

■ To make the stuffing, in a bowl combine all the ingredients except the vine leaves and oil. It should be cold and sticky enough to shape, and is enough for 24 vine leaves.

■ If the leaves are fresh, stem and wash them. Then blanch them in boiling water for 15 seconds. Strain and allow to cool. If the leaves are vacuum-packed, you will need to wash out the brine in several cold water rinses.

METHOD

■ Spread the vine leaves flat on a clean work surface. Place a spoonful of filling on each leaf and roll to produce a cylinder as shown in the diagram (the amount of filling and size of the finished dolmades will depend on the size of the leaves). Also, do not overfill them or wrap too tightly because they will swell during cooking.

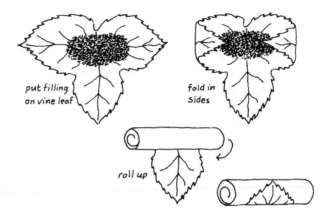

put filling on vine leaf

fold in sides

roll up

■ Preheat the oven to 300°F. To prevent the vine leaves from sticking during cooking use a nonstick pastry baking pan. If you don't have such a pan, line an ordinary one with plastic wrap (it won't melt). Brush the tray (or plastic wrap) with olive oil. Place the dolmades on it with the tip of the rolled leaf downwards. Do not squash them, just let them touch each other lightly. Brush them with olive oil, and cover the pan(s) with aluminum foil. Put into the preheated oven and cook for 20 to 30 minutes. Serve hot or cold.

Noodles with Yogurt

TUTMAJ

SERVES 4

Most of us consider pasta to be Italian (the very word pasta is Latin for "paste"), but it is thought to be the Chinese who invented it in the form of noodles over 6,000 years ago. Noodles and noodle-making methods filtered from China via the trade routes, most probably by the first century A.D. when the Silk Route to China was first established, at which time the entire Mediterranean was under Roman control. With Roman decline, pasta-making expertise centered in Italy, but isolated pockets of noodle makers remained—in particular in Turkey and Armenia. Today in the Middle East everyone enjoys all forms of pasta Italian style and pizza/pasta bars vie with the kebab houses in most Arab cities. But *tutmaj* is different. It is normally served as a soup, but it is delicious as a thick, gravied vegetable dish.

INGREDIENTS

1 pound fresh egg noodles or 1 pound tagliatelli	2/3 cup thick yogurt
	1 tablespoon corn flour
2 tablespoons sunflower or soy oil	1 egg
1/2 cup chopped onion	20 saffron threads (optional)
2 cloves garlic, chopped (optional)	salt to taste
1/2 cup vegetable stock or water	chopped mint and parsley to taste

METHOD

■ Bring 6 cups water to a boil in a large saucepan. Immerse the noodles or tagliatelli, reduce the heat, and simmer for 5 to 10 minutes. Stir, occasionally, and test to get exactly the texture you like. Strain and set aside.

■ Meanwhile, in a skillet or wok heat the oil and sauté the onion and garlic for 5 minutes.

■ In a bowl, whisk together the stock, yogurt, corn flour, egg, and saffron.

■ Add the yogurt mixture to the sautéed onion and garlic, stirring it in quickly. (The yogurt should not curdle as it is heated.)

■ Once it begins to simmer, add the noodles and combine. Season with salt and fresh mint and parsley, and serve on its own or as an accompaniment to a meat dish.

■ **N**ote: If you want it as a soup, add more stock or water when the yogurt is being added to the sautéed onions and garlic.

Yogurtlu Papyon Makarna

A Turkish variation of *tutmaj* replaces the noodles with bow-tie pasta (*fiochetti*), which are available plain or green. Simply substitute one for the other and follow the previous recipe.

Scrambled Egg with Peppers

MENEMEN

SERVES 4 AS
AN ENTRÉE

Simple and delicious, this Turkish recipe can serve as a snack, a light meal or a side dish. The quantities here will give an ample amount for four.

INGREDIENTS

1 red bell pepper	8 cherry tomatoes
1 green bell pepper	8 eggs
2 to 4 fresh chiles (optional)	aromatic salt (see page 23) and black pepper
1 tablespoon olive oil	
2 cloves garlic, chopped	chopped cilantro

METHOD

■ Stem and seed the red and green bell peppers and then chop into small diamond shapes. Slice the chiles into thin rings.

■ In a skillet or wok, heat the oil and sauté the garlic for 1 minute. Add the peppers and chiles and a splash of water to prevent them from sticking, and continue to sauté for 5 minutes. Add another splash of water and the tomatoes, and carefully cook to soften but not split them.

■ In a separate bowl, beat the eggs lightly with a fork, then pour them over the sautéed mixture. Reduce the heat. Allow the eggs to begin to set, then stir carefully until it is ready to serve. Watch that it doesn't burn and stick.

■ Season with salt and pepper and garnish with cilantro. Serve with pita bread or toast.

Herbal Omelette

KOOKOO SABZI

SERVES 4

It is slightly misleading to call this celebrated Iranian dish an omelette, because it is quite thick and firmly set and packed with green herbs, quite unlike the very light, thin, folded Western omelette. The *kookoo* has many filling variations including vegetables, potatoes, and meat.

The best way to get the texture right is to bake it in a round flan pan in the oven. Serve it as a light meal or to accompany other dishes.

The Arabian version of this dish is called *ijjah bil tawabel*. To make it simply add a pinch of sumak to the recipe here.

Kookoo now rooz (New Year's omelette) is traditionally served at the Iranian New Year. It is exactly the same as *kookoo sabzi* with the addition of chopped nuts and dried fruit, and is garnished with thick yogurt and fennel sprigs.

INGREDIENTS

1/2 cup spinach	melted clarified butter
2 bunches scallions	6 eggs
4 tablespoons chopped fresh parsley	1/4 teaspoon turmeric
4 tablespoons chopped fresh mint	20 saffron threads
1/2 tablespoon dried mint	aromatic salt (see page 23) and black pepper
4 tablespoons snipped fresh chives	1/2 teaspoon cayenne (optional)
2 tablespoons each of 3 or 4 more herbs: chervil, watercress, basil, dill, etc.	

METHOD

■ Wash the spinach, carefully removing all grit and sand. Dry, stem, and shred the leaves into fine strips.

■ Slice the scallions into thin rings, including the leaves.

■ In a bowl, toss the spinach, scallions, and herbs together and set aside.

■ Preheat the oven to 325°F. Use a flan dish 8 or 9 inches in diameter, preferably nonstick, and brush it with melted clarified butter.

■ In a separate bowl, beat the eggs with a whisk. Add the remaining ingredients and then the greens. Combine thoroughly and immediately transfer the mixture to the flan dish and cover with aluminum foil.

■ Bake for 20 minutes. Remove the foil and bake for another 10 minutes, then check it. The top should be light brown, the inside just cooked but still soft. If you want it more firm, continue to cook for a few minutes longer.

Egg-Stuffed Omelette

EGGAH MASHIYA BAIDH

SERVES 4

Nobody enjoys eggs more than the Egyptians, and no Middle Eastern cookbook would be complete without an Egyptian egg dish. My choice is this omelette, appropriately called an *eggah* in Egypt (and *agga, igga* or *ijja* in other Arabic dialects). This *eggah* has a filling of chopped hard-boiled egg (*baidh*), mixed with fresh herbs and yogurt. *Tzvazegh* are miniature spiced omelettes.

INGREDIENTS

2 tablespoons clarified butter	2 tablespoons yogurt
2 cloves garlic, chopped	1 tablespoon clarified butter or olive oil
1/4 teaspoon turmeric	4 eggs, beaten
1/4 cup chopped onion	1/2 teaspoon aromatic salt (see page 23)
4 eggs, hard-boiled and chopped	mustard greens and watercress
2 or 3 tablespoons chopped chives, mint, and parsley	

METHOD

■ To make the filling, in a skillet or wok, heat the clarified butter and sauté the garlic and turmeric for 1 minute. Add the onion and cook for another 5 minutes. Remove from the heat and stir in the chopped eggs, herbs, and yogurt. Keep warm but do not keep it on a direct heat source.

■ To make the eggahs, heat the clarified butter in a large flat frying pan. Salt the eggs and pour half into the pan. Cook on medium heat until set, then turn over and cook for another 1 or 2 minutes, until dried to taste.

■ Turn the eggah out onto a plate. Spread half the warm filling onto half the eggah. Fold over and keep warm.

■ Repeat the steps for the second omelette.

■ To serve, cut each eggah in half and garnish with mustard greens and watercress.

THE STAPLES

▲▲▲▲▲▲▲▲▲▲▲▲▲▲▲▲▲▲

Grains, or the seeds of certain grasses such as barley, corn, maize, millet, oats, rye, wheat and rice, have become essential or "staple" foods. In areas where drought has always been a common occurrence, the importance of grain throughout history can be measured by frequent written evidence of its suitability for long-term storage. The Bible refers to the years of plenty when the grain stores were filled to bursting, and of famine when supplies were exhausted. The Pharaohs took vessels of grain with them into the pyramids on their passage to the afterlife.

Wheat in the form of bread has, for millennia, been "the staff of life" to the peoples of the Mediterranean. Rice, too, is called the "staff of life" by the Iranians, who also refer to it as "the soul of Allah."

WHEAT

About 12,000 years ago, when man began to cultivate the land of the Fertile Crescent, one of the first major crops was wheat. It was eaten in a fairly unrefined form, but eventually a process was developed to make it more palatable. The wheat grain was cracked, partly cooked, dried in the sun, and then ground. It was stored until required, when it was reconstituted with water in a porridge-like form. It was probably mankind's first processed food. Today, known as bulgur, it is still used in Middle Eastern recipes, particularly the meat stews and salads of Syria and Lebanon.

Wheat grows in many of the countries of the Middle East. Barley, oats, and rye are grown in North Africa and Greece, maize in Morocco, Egypt, and Turkey.

Processed Semolina Grains

COUSCOUS

SERVES 4

Couscous is the ancient staple of the Maghreb in North Africa, and was undoubtedly the invention of the original inhabitants of the area, the Berbers. Just when can never be known, but it is likely to have been after 2500 B.C., when the Berbers became isolated from the Egyptians, and before 1000 B.C., by which time wheat had become the bread-making staple in Egypt. We can say this with some certainty because couscous has remained almost exclusively in the Maghreb (reflecting the isolation of the Berbers in the following millennia) and because both bread and the staple that the Arabs brought from India—rice—did not become part of Maghrebi cuisine until around A.D. 900.

The Berbers may well have been regarded throughout history as primitive hill people, but there is nothing primitive about the preparation of couscous. It requires great skill, and for that reason it is better to use one of the very excellent commercial brands. Specifically it is made from semolina, which itself is coarsely ground *durum* (hard) wheat. To make couscous, grains of semolina are spread out, sprinkled with water, and rolled with the fingertips with a further sprinkling of fine white flour. The new larger grains are sieved to achieve a constant size (which can vary from small to large). The grains are steamed in a special steamer called a *couscousière,* which is a double boiler with a large, water-boiling base and snugly fitting slotted top unit with equally snug-fitting lid. Traditionally these were (and still are) made from pottery, but can also be brass or its modern equivalent, aluminum. When the water is boiling the couscous is placed on muslin in the top unit. The lid is put on and the couscous is steamed for 30 minutes, being aerated by forking it from time to time. It is then removed and spread out in a thin layer on muslin to dry in the hot sun for two days. The dry grains can then be stored indefinitely, and it is in this form that we can buy couscous as a product.

Standard couscous consists of creamy pellets resembling sesame seeds in size and appearance and they must be steamed again, this time with a savory stew in the bottom which imparts its flavors into the grains. The final dish is served with the strained stew at the center of a nest of couscous, and the strained gravy separate. The dish (also called couscous) can be meat- or fish-based, see pages 73, 74, and 102.

This recipe details the steaming of couscous grains.

INGREDIENTS

1 pound commercial couscous (see note below)	**1 teaspoon aromatic salt (see page 23)**
2 tablespoons clarified butter	

133

METHOD

■ If you don't have a double-boiler, use a large, deep saucepan in which fits very snugly a close-mesh strainer, about 8 inches in diameter to allow ample water to boil without the strainer touching it. Following the directions on your store-bought couscous package, bring the water to a boil.

■ Rinse the couscous briefly. Strain well and spread out in a large tray to dry.

■ When the water has boiled, check that the grains are separate. Line the strainer with a clean tea towel or muslin, and put the strainer into the saucepan. Use the flaps of the tea towel under the strainer to ensure that no steam escapes. Once steam is flowing through the tea towel, trickle half the couscous onto it and fit the lid tightly. Leave for 3 or 4 minutes, by which time it will be well steamed. Then loosen it with a spoon. Trickle the remaining couscous in and refit the lid. Once the steam is flowing through the couscous, turn the heat down to achieve an effective simmer.

■ Every few minutes, aerate the couscous by loosening with a fork. Continue to steam for 20 to 25 minutes (adding water as needed).

■ In a separate container heat the meat or fish accompaniment (see pages 73, 74, and 102).

■ When the couscous has steamed, remove it from the heat. Empty it into the flat tray and add the clarified butter and salt, working it in with the fingertips. Pour away any remaining water from the saucepan. Then put the hot meat or vegetable accompaniment into the couscous saucepan, ensuring there is enough liquid to enable it to simmer for about 20 minutes.

■ Replace the tea towel or muslin in the strainer and put the couscous back in and the strainer over the simmering water.

■ Simmer for another 20 minutes, aerating the couscous.

■ Before serving be sure that the couscous grains are separate. Make a mound of the couscous on a platter and make a depression in the mound.

■ Strain the accompanying sauce and put the solids into the depression. Serve the sauce in a gravy boat, allowing the diners to add the amount of their choice.

Note: There are many different brands of commercial couscous and all are of perfectly acceptable quality. Most have recipes which state boil the couscous rather than the above steaming. It can be boiled, but this never cooks it to fluffiness in the way that steaming does. In some cases, where the couscous has been precooked, it will require considerably less steaming time than given above. Taste and test it regularly after five minutes, or follow the instructions on the packet.

Rice

Rice originated in China and India, where it has been eaten for at least 9,000 years. The Middle East does not enjoy enough humidity and rainfall to allow for widespread cultivation of rice, but rice has become a fundamental part of the region's cuisine since it was introduced from India via Iran over 2,500 years ago. It was the Arabs who ensured its spread into North Africa and Spain by the ninth century. Later the Venetians, the Arabs' Mediterranean trading partners, took rice to Italy.

Rice grows in small quantities along the northern Nile in Egypt and in the Anatolia area of Turkey. Iran is self-sufficient in rice production, most of it being farmed in the north. Three of the best-quality Iranian extra long-grained rices are *champa*, *berenje sadri* and *dom siyah* (black-tailed). They are superb for cooking and occasionally they can be found in specialty shops in the West. The rice that is widely used in the Middle East is basmati rice, imported from India and Pakistan.

The Iranian dish *pollou* or pillau (from *pollo*, rice), is a combination of basmati rice cooked by absorption with spices and meat or poultry or vegetables. This dish was taken east to India, where pullao rice and pullao dishes are some of the most important rice dishes of the subcontinent. Westwards, this most famous Persian dish became the basis of *pilav* or *pilaf* in Turkey and Armenia, as well as the *pilafi* dishes of Greece and the paellas of Spain. Steamed plain rice is called *timman* in Iraq, and a similar dish in the Levant area is called *riz mulfalfel*. The North African group of countries—Tunisia, Algeria and Morocco—do not have a rice-eating tradition, preferring couscous (see page 133). Our own word "rice" is derived from the Arabic *riz* or *roz*, itself from an ancient word *aruz*. The Hindi word for rice is *chawal*, and the Afghanistan *chaulau* and the Iranian *chellow* are derived from that.

Rice accompanies many Middle Eastern dishes. It is usually enhanced with smen (clarified butter) and spices, or it is mixed with other ingredients such as lentils, meat, vegetables, or even pasta noodles. Occasionally though, it is nice to have unspiced (plain) rice, especially with rich dishes.

There are two basic methods for cooking rice: One consists of boiling it in plenty of water and then draining, and the other of cooking it in a precisely measured amount of water which is completely absorbed by the rice. Both methods give individual and fluffy grains of rice, both can be spiced or unspiced, and both take around the same amount of time to cook. The rice grains swell to a slightly larger size with the boiling method, and they are softer. Using the absorption method, the spicing is cooked in from the early stages of cooking and it is marginally more flavorful.

Basmati rice is a long, narrow-grained, fragrant rice, hard enough to retain a superb al dente bite when cooked. All the timings for the recipes which follow are for basmati rice. Other long-grained or fast-cooking rices may require different cooking times and most are unlikely to give the fluffiness and fragrance of basmati.

Plain Rice by Boiling

SERVES 4

This is the quickest way to cook rice, and it can be ready to serve in just 15 minutes from the time the water boils. Two factors are crucial for this method to work perfectly, however. First, the rice *must* be basmati rice. Patna or long-grained, quick-cooking or other rices will require different timings and will have neither the texture nor the fragrance of basmati. Second, it is one of the few recipes in this book which requires precision timing. It is essential that for its few minutes on the boil you concentrate on it or else it may overcook and become starchy.

A 1/3-cup portion of dry rice provides an ample helping per person: 1/4 cup will be a smaller but adequate portion.

INGREDIENTS

1 1/2 cups basmati or other long-grained rice	3 cups water

METHOD

- Pick through the rice to remove any grit and particles.

- In a saucepan, bring the water to a boil. It is not necessary to salt it.

- While the water is heating, rinse the rice with fresh cold water until most of the starch is washed out. Run hot tap water through the rice at the final rinse. This minimizes the temperature reduction of the boiling water when the rice is added to it.

- When the water is boiling, add the rice and start timing. Put the lid on the pan until the water returns to a boil, then remove. It takes 8 to 10 minutes from the start. Stir frequently.

- After about 6 minutes, taste a few grains. As soon as the center is no longer brittle, but still has a good al dente bite to it, strain off the water. The rice should seem slightly *under*cooked.

- Shake off all excess water, then place the strainer onto a dry tea towel which will help remove the last of the water.

- After a minute place the rice in a prewarmed serving dish. Serve it immediately or put it into a warm oven for about 30 minutes. As it dries, the grains will separate and become fluffy. It can be kept in the warm oven for several hours.

Plain Rice by Absorption

SERVES 4

Cooking rice by a premeasured ratio of rice to water which is all absorbed into the rice is undoubtedly the best way to do it. Provided that you use basmati rice, the finished grains are longer, thinner, and much more fragrant and flavorful than they are after boiling.

The method is actually very easy, but many cookbooks make it sound far too complicated. Instructions invariably state that you must use a tightly lidded pot and precise water quantity and heat levels, and never lift the lid during the boiling process, etc. However, I lift the lid, I stir the rice, and I've even cooked rice by absorption without a lid. If I've erred on the side of too little water, I've added a bit during "the boil." (Too much water, however, is an unresolvable problem.) In other words, I've broken all the rules, but it still seems to work.

Another myth propagated in other cookbooks is the time factor. They tend to say that rice must be served as soon as "the boil" is completed. This causes stress to the cook who believes that there is no margin of error in time and method. In reality, the longer you give the rice to dry, the fluffier and more fragrant it will be. So it can be cooked well in advance of being required for serving. After the initial "boil" and 10-minute simmer the rice is quite sticky, and it needs to "relax." After 30 minutes it can be served and is fluffy, but it can be kept in a warm place for much longer—and the fluffiness only improves.

Cooking rice by this method does need practice. But don't be intimidated and don't give up. Here are some tips for the novice:

Choose a pan, preferably with a lid, that can be used both on the stove and in the oven. Until you have had lots of practice, always use the same pan, so that you become familiar with it.

Keep an eye on the clock. The timing of "the boil" is important or you'll burn the bottom of the rice.

Always use basmati rice. It won't let you down.

If you intend to let the rice cool down for serving later or the next day, or even to freeze it, do not put it in the warmer. It is better slightly under-cooked for these purposes.

INGREDIENTS

1 1/2 cups basmati rice	3 cups water

METHOD

- Soak the rice in extra water to cover for about 30 minutes.

- Rinse it until the rinse water runs more or less clear, then strain.

137

METHOD

■ Bring the measured water to a boil in a saucepan (as heavy as possible, and with a lid), or a casserole dish at least twice the volume of the strained rice.

■ As soon as it is boiling add the rice and stir in well.

■ As soon as it starts bubbling, put the lid on the pan and reduce the heat by half and leave alone for 8 minutes.

■ Check the rice. If all the liquid has been absorbed, remove from the heat. If not, replace the lid and leave for 2 more minutes. When the liquid has been absorbed, stir the rice well so that it does not stick to the bottom. Taste it. It should not be brittle in the middle. If it is, add a little more water and heat for a little longer.

■ Place the saucepan or casserole in an oven preheated to its very lowest setting. You can serve the rice at once, but the longer you leave it, the more separate the grains will be. An hour is fine, but it will be quite safe if left for several hours.

Fried Rice Iraqi-Style

TIMMAN

SERVES 4

This dish is called *riz m'falfal* in Lebanon, *beyaz pilav* (white rice) in Turkey and *dami* in Iran.

INGREDIENTS

rice (see method)	1/2 teaspoon aromatic salt (see page 23)
2 tablespoons clarified butter	

SERVES 4

BOILING METHOD

METHOD

■ Follow the recipe for "plain rice by boiling" on page 136.

■ When the rice is ready to serve, wash and dry the saucepan and heat the clarified butter in it. Put the rice and salt in and sauté for a couple of minutes, until it is warm. Serve immediately or keep it in a warm oven for up to several hours.

SERVES 4

ABSORPTION METHOD

METHOD

- Follow the recipe for "plain rice by absorption" on page 137 through soaking and rinsing the rice.

- In a saucepan, bring the water to a boil.

- In another saucepan (as heavy as possible and with a lid), or a casserole dish at least twice the volume of the strained rice, heat the clarified butter.

- Add the rice and the salt and sauté about 2 minutes, making sure that the oil coats the rice and that it heats through. Add the boiled water and combine thoroughly with the rice.

- Then follow the rest of the instructions for cooking "plain rice by absorption."

Crusty Iranian Rice

CHELLOW

SERVES 4

This dish was being eaten in Persia 3,000 years ago and it is still regarded as Iran's most important rice dish. It must be cooked by the absorption method, not only to achieve the best flavors, but to create a crust on the bottom of the cooking pot. Called *tahdig* in Iranian or *hakkakah* in Arabic, the crust is regarded as the best part of the rice, rather like the crusty end of fresh bread, and it is always offered to guests. I use a little more rice for this recipe to allow for some wastage in making the crust.

INGREDIENTS

2 cups basmati rice	1/2 teaspoon aromatic salt (see page 23)
1 tablespoon clarified butter	20 saffron threads (optional)

METHOD

- Follow the timman rice by absorption method on page 139 to the point when all of the liquid has been absorbed. Do not stir the rice at any stage, otherwise the crust won't form at the bottom of the pan. Apply full heat to the pan for 2 to 3 minutes, then either serve immediately or place in a warm oven until ready to serve.

- To serve, remove the fluffy rice first, carefully teasing it off the crust. Then scrape the crust from the pan bottom. Not everyone likes this Iranian delicacy, so offer it on a separate plate.

Rice Crust

TAHDIG OR HAKKAKAH

A variation on *chellow* is to grate peeled raw potato and fry it in the saucepan before adding the rice as in the *timman* recipe on page 138. When the potatoes are cooked, add the rice, but don't stir it into the potatoes. Then add the boiled water and proceed with the recipe instructions.

Iranian Rice

POLLOU

SERVES 4

Pollous are another delightful Iranian specialty. The rice is cooked with a choice of fragrant spices and clarified butter. Pollous often include meat or fish or vegetables in the cooking, but here the recipe calls for only aromatic spices. It can be cooked by the boiling method (see page 136), with fried spices being added at the end, or by the absorption method (see page 137), frying the spices before adding the water.

INGREDIENTS

1 1/2 cups basmati rice	1/2 teaspoon white cumin seeds
4 to 6 cups water (boiling method)	1/4 teaspoon black cumin seeds
4 tablespoons clarified butter	1/4 teaspoon fennel seeds
4 green cardamoms	1 2-inch piece cassia bark
4 cloves	20 saffron threads

SERVES 4

BOILING METHOD

METHOD

■ Follow the recipe for "plain rice by boiling" on page 136 to the point of removing the rice from the saucepan to drain.

■ Rinse and dry the saucepan or casserole dish, and heat the clarified butter. Sauté the spices for no more than 30 seconds. Add the rice and sauté about 2 minutes until it is warmed through. Serve immediately or keep in a warm oven until ready to serve. Add the saffron just before serving.

ABSORPTION METHOD

SERVES 4

METHOD

- Follow the recipe for "plain rice by absorption" on page 137 through soaking and rinsing the rice.

- In a separate pan, boil the water.

- In a saucepan (as heavy as possible and with a lid), or a casserole dish at least twice the volume of the strained rice, heat the clarified butter. Sauté the spices for no more than 30 seconds.

- Add the rice and continue to sauté about 2 minutes, making sure the oil coats the rice and that it heats through. Add the boiling water and stir it well into the rice.

- Then complete the instructions for the method for plain rice by absorption, adding the saffron just before serving.

Rice with Vermicelli

ROZ BI SHA'RIYAH

SERVES 4

The combination of grain with pasta may seem unlikely, but it is one of the most popular dishes in the Mediterranean Middle East. This dish goes back to the Middle Ages, devised at a time when Arab links with Venice were at their height. Rice was traded to Italy, pasta returned to the East. One mixed marriage was this Jordanian recipe.

INGREDIENTS

1 cup basmati rice	3 tablespoons clarified butter
1/2 cup vermicelli	3 tablespoons pine nuts, roasted

METHOD

- Follow the recipe for "plain rice by absorption" on page 137 through soaking and rinsing the rice.

- Break the vermicelli into 1-inch pieces.

- In a separate pan, bring the water to a boil.

- In a saucepan (as heavy as possible, with a lid), or a casserole dish at least twice the volume of the rice and vermicelli, heat the clarified butter.

METHOD
- Add the rice and vermicelli and sauté about 2 minutes, making sure the oil coats the rice and vermicelli and that they heat through. Add the boiled water and continue to sauté, combining thoroughly.

- Then continue to follow the instruction for the method of "plain rice by absorption." Garnish with pine nuts.

Rice with Dates

RIZ EL TAMMAR

SERVES 4

Libya's principal culinary asset is the date—in fact dozens of species of date—and Libyans traditionally consume more rice than their Maghrebi neighbors. Together they make for a dish of great character, to accompany savory dishes.

INGREDIENTS

1 1/2 cups basmati rice	1/2 teaspoon aromatic salt (see page 23)
1/4 cup dates. pitted and chopped	2 tablespoons clarified butter
2 teaspoons orange-blossom water	1 tablespoon pistachio nuts

METHOD
- Cook the rice either by the boiling method on page 136 or by absorption on page 137.

- With either method, add the remaining ingredients and mix them in well after the cooking stage and prior to the rice "resting."

Bread

The ancient Egyptians mastered the art of fermentation to make wine and beer some 4,000 years ago. They also discovered how to ferment dough (leavening), and developed the baking of bread. By 1500 B.C. round flat loaves, called *aiysh*, were sold in bakeries. *Aiysh* in Egyptian means "life," and bread has long been called "the staff (support) of life." The importance of bread remains undiminished, with the method of baking aiysh unchanged to this day, and similar bread is to be found all over the Middle East. Shapes and sizes vary from discs of around 6 inches to ovals of 8 to 10 inches, but the basic dough is the same. This type of bread is called *khoubiz* or *khubz* in Arabia and the Levant; *kmaj* in Lebanon (with pocket) or *mafroudha* (without); *saluf* in Yemen; *shrak* in Jordan and Palestine, and *aiysh shami* in Syria. In Israel it is called *matzo*, and in Greece it is *taftoon*. A larger, oval Iranian variety is called *nane lavash*, which is the derivative of the celebrated *naan* bread of India. Equally well known is the pita of Greece and Turkey. In Morocco the standard bread is *khobz* made from unleavened plain white flour and rolled into round flat discs about 12 inches in diameter and 2 inches high. Unique to Morocco is *hasha* or *matlou*, a leavened bread made from semolina, and *ksra*, also leavened and made from semolina but mixed with flour and spiced with sesame and aniseed.

There are many other types of bread to be found in the Middle East, such as the Iranian *barbari*. Made from white flour, it is 2 inches long and 4 inches wide after baking with four ribs. The *sangyak*, also from Iran, is 2 feet 6 inches wide, oiled on top and baked on hot pebbles until it bubbles. Yemen produces two breads of distinction—*maluj* from a barley dough, and *bint-al-sahn*, where sheets of thinly rolled yeasty dough are spread with samneh (see page 21), placed in layers one on top of the other, then baked. Israel's bagels and pretzels are especially well known in bakeries of modern Israel, as well as those of Jewish communities all over the world. *Samouli* is a type of Arabian French loaf stick, varying in size from very short to quite long. A variation of the bagel appears as *samit* in Egypt, *kaak* in the Levant, and *simit* in Turkey. It is a sesame seed-sprinkled, golden-baked ring popular at breakfast with yogurt and honey. *Korek* or *charek* is a tea-time sweet bun containing raisins, sugar, milk, and oil in the dough. It originated in Turkey but can be found all over the region. Many breads are made with a stuffing or topping. Olives are mixed into the dough of the *zeytin* in Turkey, where they also make a cake-like bread from corn flour and yogurt. Onions, herbs, chiles, and cheese can also be used as a spicy topping, spread on before baking—for example, the Yemeni *hilbeh* with fenugreek and coriander paste (see page 36).

Dough Making

Basically, once you have mastered this simple dough recipe you can make all the breads in this chapter. The secrets of success lie in the first kneading, which must achieve a thorough blending of the ingredients, and a good proofing (rising) time in a warm place. The dough should be elastic without being sticky, and it should feel satisfying to handle in that it is pliable, springy, and soft.

Dough Mix

INGREDIENTS

2 tablespoons fresh yeast	4 cups strong white flour (huwmara), brown chapatti flour (khashkar), or whole-wheat flour
water	

METHOD

- Dissolve the fresh yeast in a little warm water.

- Place the flour in a warmed bowl, make a well in the center, and pour in the dissolved yeast (or 2 tablespoons plain yogurt can be used in the absence of yeast).

- Gently mix into the flour, and add enough tepid water to make a firm dough.

- Remove from the bowl and knead on a floured board until well combined. Return the dough to the bowl and leave in a warm place, covered with a towel, for a couple of hours to rise. Your dough, when risen, should have doubled in size. It should be bubbly and stringy, like elastic.

- Punch down the dough by kneading it down to its original size. Add the recipe spices.

- Proceed to the recipe of your choice from the following pages.

Arab Bread

KHOUBIZ OR KHOBZ

MAKES 4
LOAVES

Khoubiz is the standard, flat, slightly leavened bread to be found all over the Levant and the Gulf, and as far afield as Morocco (where it is called *khobz*) and the other Maghreb countries. In Jordan and Palestine the identical bread is called *sh'raak*. Basically, khoubiz is a round, flat disc varying in size from country to country between 6 inches and 12 inches in diameter. Khoubiz has been made for thousands of years, and the only change is the recent option of using white flour (*huwmara*). Finely ground whole-wheat flour (*khashkar*), using a hard wheat grain, is traditional. Western whole-wheat flour suffices, but, if you can get it, use chapatti flour.

INGREDIENTS

1 quantity of white or brown dough (see
    page 144)

METHOD

■ Follow the dough-making recipe on page 144.

■ Divide the dough into 4 equal pieces and shape into balls. Roll each into a disc about 9 inches in diameter. Let stand to proof while preheating the oven to 400°F.

■ Arrange the discs on floured baking sheets. Prick them with a fork to prevent them rising, then bake for 8 to 10 minutes. Serve hot.

Lebanese Spicy Bread

MAN'AIYSH OR MN'AQISH

Here the standard khoubiz bread is rolled into discs about 5 inches in diameter by 1/4 inch thick. The disc is made slightly concave, then liberally brushed with a mixture of olive oil and za'atar before being baked. Prick the discs to prevent them from puffing up.

Syrian Onion Bread

KHOUBIZ BASALI

Identical to the above, but the topping is minced raw onion mixed with a little ground cumin and coriander and dried mint.

Yemeni Spicy Bread

SALUF BI HILBEH

Yemeni people adore spices almost as much as the Indians. In this case spread the disc with *hilbeh* (see page 36), then bake as usual.

Greek/Turkish Oval Bread

PITA BREAD

MAKES 6

Probably the most celebrated bread from the Middle East is the pita, that delicious, oval-shaped, flat bread with the pocket, so convenient for holding food. Pita is, in fact, simply a variant of khoubiz, the main difference being in its shape. Indeed in Syria it is called *khubz shami* or *aiysh shami*, while in the Gulf it is called *khubz arabi*. The traditional pita shape is an oval about 8 x 6 inches and 3/16 inch (2–3 mm) thick. It must always have a pocket, known as *mutbag*.

Pitas are easy enough to make, and the way to achieve the pocket is to knead the dough well, leaving it to rise and expand in a warm place, and then bake in a hot oven. If the pocket is not required, prick the rolled-out bread with a fork. An Armenian variation of pita is *pideh*: it uses whole-wheat flour, and white sesame seeds are pressed onto the dough before baking.

INGREDIENTS

1 quantity of dough (see page 144)

METHOD

■ Follow the dough-making recipe on page 144.

■ Divide the dough into 6 pieces and then roll into oval shapes as described above. Let stand to proof while preheating the oven to 400°F.

■ Arrange the discs on floured baking sheets, and bake for 8 to 10 minutes. Serve hot.

Egyptian Bread

AIYSH

Follow the previous recipe exactly, using a brown dough. Shape into 4 discs of about 6 to 8 inches in diameter and 1 inch thick. When cooked, the *aiysh* puffs up like a balloon and it should be quite soft, which is ideal for scooping up food.

Barbari

IRANIAN WHITE BREAD

MAKES 8 LOAVES

Barbari is rectangular in shape and can vary in size from 2 x 4 inches to 6 x 12 inches. It traditionally has 4 ribs or grooves, which are made by scoring with a knife. I prefer to make them small as they look so attractive. They are usually unspiced, but they can be brushed with either sesame, cumin, or caraway seeds before baking.

INGREDIENTS

1 quantity of white dough (see page 144)

METHOD

■ Follow the dough-making recipe on page 144.

■ Divide the dough into 8 pieces. Shape them into small rectangles, then roll them out to 2 x 4 inches x 1/2 inch thick. Score them on the top almost completely through 4 times with a sharp knife. Arrange them on floured baking sheets, allowing room between each for expansion during proofing. Let stand to proof while preheating the oven to 400°F.

■ Bake for 8 to 10 minutes. Serve hot.

Arabian Crisp Bread

RAGAYIG

MAKES 8 LOAVES

The recipe for this completely unleavened bread most certainly predates aiysh, khoubiz, and pita, and probably originated when man first learned to cultivate wheat over 9,000 years ago. The dough is very simple, being made from whole-wheat or all-purpose flour and water. It is kneaded and rolled into thin discs, which are baked slowly at the local bakers (*furunji*) for a few pennies, or they are cooked over charcoal on a *sorj* (an inverted cast-iron, wok-like implement). When cooked, the discs are eaten at once or they are further dried in the sun to crisp them. After this treatment they can be stored in a lidded earthenware pot for months. An Iranian variation is called *lavash* and in Turkey it is *kavgir*.

INGREDIENTS

1 quantity of brown or white dough, yeast
    omitted (see page 144)

METHOD

■ Mix the flour and enough warm water in a bowl to make a firm dough.

■ Remove from the bowl and knead on a clean, floured work surface until well combined. Return to the bowl and leave the dough for half an hour or so. It won't rise, but it will have a better elasticity.

■ Divide the dough into 8 pieces and roll out into discs around 9 inches diameter by 1/8 inch thick. Place the disc on floured baking sheets and bake in the oven at 400°F for 10 to 12 minutes. When cool, they can be broken into pieces and stored like biscuits in an airtight container. If they lose their crispness, rebake for a few minutes.

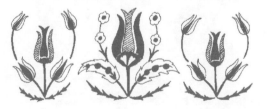

Lebanese Sweet Lenten Bread

PAKTAKATA

MAKES 4 LOAVES

This delightful "surprise" bread is traditionally made only during Lent by the small Christian community in the Levant. The dough contains syrup or honey and is rolled out into a thick disc about 6 inches in diameter and 1/2 inch thick. The surface of the disc is often highly decorated with shapes and squiggles made by running the tip of a knife or fork over it. Buried inside the dough is a clean silver coin (it's rather like the English Christmas pudding tradition), and the children vie with each other to get the coins— and that's the surprise.

INGREDIENTS

1 quantity of white dough (see page 144)	4 clean "silver" coins
1 1/2 to 2 tablespoons honey	

METHOD

- Follow the dough-making recipe on page 144, adding the honey to the yeast and water.

- Divide the dough into 4 equal pieces and shape into balls. Place one coin into the center of each ball, then roll each out to discs as above. Decorate them as you wish. Place them on floured baking sheets.

- Bake for 10 to 12 minutes in the preheated, 400°F oven. Serve hot.

Jewish Crusty Bread Rings

BAGELS

MAKES 16 BAGELS

Bagels have been popularized by Jewish communities the world over. They are golden brown, hard crusty rings, said to have been created by a Polish Jew in the Middle Ages to celebrate the winning of a major war. Be that as it may, they are now as popular in Israel as they are elsewhere. The unusual feature of bagel cooking is that the rings are blanched in boiling water (which removes starch and makes the bagel lighter) before they are baked. Bagels can be baked with a variety of toppings including chopped onion, sesame seeds, blue poppy seeds, raisins, and honey.

INGREDIENTS

1 quantity of white dough (see page 144)	1/2 teaspoon salt
1 egg	1 egg, beaten
2 teaspoons sugar	sesame seeds
2 tablespoons clarified butter or butter	

METHOD

- Follow the dough-making recipe on page 144, adding the egg, sugar, clarified butter or butter, and salt at the end of the process.

- Divide the dough into 4 equal pieces and then subdivide each piece into another 4 pieces to create 16 equal portions of dough.

- Roll one piece of dough into a cylinder of about 8 inches in length and 1/2 inch thickness. Curl into a ring, ensuring that the join is very secure. Repeat with the other 15 portions. Leave the rings to proof in a warm place for about 15 minutes.

- Preheat the oven to 400°F and bring a pan of water (about 4 cups) to a boil on the stove.

- Immerse one ring in the boiling water. When it rises to the surface (1 or 2 minutes), remove it, and put it on a floured or greased baking sheet. Repeat with the other rings.

- Glaze each ring with the beaten egg and sprinkle with sesame seeds or other topping.

- Bake for 15 minutes, by which time they should be a nice golden color.

Crusty Bread Rings

KA'AK

Variations of the bagel are found in many Middle Eastern countries. In Tunisia and Libya they are called *ka'kis* or *ka'kis bil semsem*; in the Levant *ka'ak*; in Armenia *choerig*; and in Egypt *semit*. In other countries *semit* are ring-shaped, but thicker than *ka'ak*. In Turkey *semit* street-sellers carry the rings around on long poles. In Armenia the *choerig* has evolved from a ring into a snail shape. In all other respects it is the same as *semit*.

METHOD

■ To make *ka'ak* or *choerig* follow the bagel recipe. Add 1 teaspoon *mahlab* to the dough mix (see page 144).

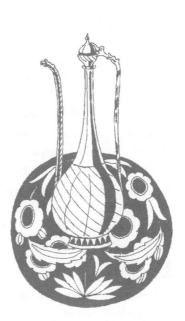

151

DESSERTS AND SWEET THINGS

▲▲▲▲▲▲▲▲▲▲▲▲▲▲▲▲

To say that the people of the Middle East have a sweet tooth is an understatement. Probably the most celebrated Middle Eastern sweet pastries are baklava and kadayif, which are made from the thinnest filo pastry—baklava in layers, kadayif in shredded form—and drenched in sticky sweet syrup. My selection of recipes here includes both of these, as well as a selection of puddings including *m'hancha* (the intriguing Moroccan pastry "snake cake," so called because it is curled like a sleeping serpent) and *irmik helvasi* from Turkey (fried semolina pudding called *sujee helva* in the Levant). Pancakes are represented by two ultra-tasty recipes—blintze from Israel, and *ataif* from Bahrain.

A dessert with a delightful name—*um m'ali* (Ali's mom's pudding)—is in fact a rather excellent bread and butter pudding. And no Middle Eastern sweet chapter would be complete without a recipe using the prolific date.

If none of these take your fancy you may want to provide something simpler. Fresh fruit is an obvious and always welcome choice. Indigenous to the Middle East, and amongst the earliest fruit to be cultivated, was the apple. The grape, pomegranate, fig, date, cherry, and pear are equally ancient. Apricots and peaches originated in China, and had reached the Middle East centuries before Christ. Oranges, also from China, came later. From India in the early trading days came guavas, bananas, mangos, limes and melons. The only major fruit to have been introduced to the Arab world from America was the strawberry.

Ice cream is very popular all over the Middle East and can be made with water (sorbet style), with milk, and with thick rich cream, so it is quite legitimate to serve with any Middle Eastern menu, if for no other reason than for its Arabic name—*booza-booza*!

Sweet Crisp Pastries

BAKLAVA

ENOUGH FOR
12 TO 18
SERVINGS

Baklava is undoubtedly one of the most celebrated and best-known sweet pastries from the Middle East. It is readily available in Greek, Turkish, and Middle Eastern restaurants and delicatessens all over the world. Each baklava is a diamond-shaped assembly of layered pastry, filled with dots of chopped nuts and butter, then cooked to a gorgeous golden color. It is laced with a sticky syrup and is served cold. Needless to say, it is high in calories and completely irresistible. The ancient Greeks had a dish along these lines, but it is certain that once again, as with *boreks*, it was the chefs of the Ottomans who developed it into the superb treat that it is today. It is found all over the Middle East with occasional variations in spelling (e.g., *baglavah, b'learwa*).

Delicious though it is, the commercial version is sometimes rather soggy because it has sat marinating in its syrup for two or three days. It can also be too sweet. The home-made version is easy enough to make provided you don't let the filo pastry dry out. Even made the day before, it will be much crisper than its commercial counterpart.

Make the syrup first so that it is already chilled and ready to use.

INGREDIENTS

SYRUP

1 cup water

1 cup white sugar

2 tablespoons honey (optional)

1 tablespoon lemon juice

1 teaspoon rose water or orange-blossom
  water

1 package commercial filo pastry

1 cup clarified butter

FILLING

1 1/4 cups minced pistachios, walnuts,
  hazelnuts, or almonds, mixed with 2
  teaspoons powdered cinnamon

METHOD

■ To make the syrup, bring the water to a boil in a medium saucepan. Add the sugar, and honey, if desired, stir until the sugar dissolves, then continue to stir for the next 10 minutes as it thickens to pouring consistency. Then remove from the heat. Stir in the lemon juice and rose water or orange-blossom water. Refrigerate for at least 2 hours. If the syrup thickens too much as it chills, add a little cold water to thin it.

■ Preheat the oven to 350°F. Melt the clarified butter in a small pan. Use a baking sheet about 12 x 10 inches with sides at least 2 inches high. Brush it with melted clarified butter.

153

METHOD

- Have a damp, clean tea towel at hand. Open the filo package. Trim the entire bunch of sheets to the size of the baking sheet. Cover the sheets with the tea towel to stop the filo from drying out (which it does very fast). Note: If the packet size is the standard 12 x 20 inches halve it to 12 x 10 inches and repack the spare half in a plastic bag for future use.

- Take one sheet of filo (cover the rest), and lay it on the baking sheet. Brush it with the melted clarified butter. Repeat this step with the next 5 sheets, laying each sheet gently on top of each other. This will result in a lighter pastry. After 5 sheets are stacked, sprinkle with a generous coating of the spiced nuts.

- Repeat the above step 3 more times, using all the sheets in the package.

- Traditionally baklava is cut into diamond shapes (see below). This is partly done now and is finished after cooking. Cut from the top sheet but not right through to the bottom; go about two-thirds down.

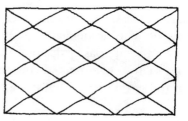

- Bake for 30 minutes, then check. It should now be pale gold in color. Increase the heat to 425°F and bake for 10 to 15 more minutes. Check during this time and remove when it is a deep golden color.

- Keep the baklava on the baking sheet and immediately finish cutting into individual pieces. Without delay pour the cold syrup onto the piping hot pastry. This achieves maximum penetration of the syrup.

- Cool in the refrigerator (for at least 3 hours), after which it can be served. Baklavas will keep in the refrigerator for 3 to 4 days.

Kadayif or Kunafah

SWEET, CRISP, SHREDDED PASTRIES

SERVES 4

Kadayif is a variation of the previous baklava recipe, and is equally well known and loved. Indeed, some people prefer it to baklava. The dough is a finely shredded filo, its strands as thin as vermicelli. It vaguely resembles shredded wheat in appearance but not in taste or color.

There are several variations of this delicious pastry—*kunafah bil eishta* is topped with thick Arab clotted cream, *kunafah bil jibn* is topped with *peynir* cheese, and *balurieh* is the Syrian version and is slowly baked at a low oven temperature so that it is a creamy white rather than a deep golden color.

If filo is hard to make at home, *kadayif* dough is almost impossible. Filo dough is watered down to batter consistency. It is then poured swiftly through a special sieve in spirals onto a huge hot griddle pan. The large white lattice is deftly scooped up and gently folded while it is still soft. It is in this form that it can be bought in 1-pound 2-ounce packages from delicatessens.

INGREDIENTS

1 package commercial kadayif dough	syrup, as for baklava (see page 153)
1/2 cup clarified butter	filling, as for baklava (see page 153)

METHOD

- Preheat the oven, melt the clarified butter, and grease a baking sheet as for baklava (see page 153).

- Open the kadayif package. Tease out the strands of dough, and halve it. Arrange one half on the baking sheet, covering the second half with a damp, clean tea towel. Without pressing it down, fit it onto the baking sheet. Brush melted clarified butter into as many of the strands as possible, working it in with your fingers. Then pour the nuts over it and gently spread them through the dough.

- Place the remaining half of the pastry on top, again buttering as many strands as possible. Gently shape it to fit on the baking sheet.

- Bake in the oven as for baklava.

- Remove from the oven and immediately pour the syrup over the hot pastry as for baklava.

- Serve hot or cold, cutting into individual portions as required.

Almond Snake Cake

EL M'HANCHA

**SERVES 4
(OR MORE)**

The Moroccan snake cake appears at any special occasion. *Warkah* pastry (or filo) is used and it is stuffed with almond paste rolled into a very long cylinder, then coiled round and round into a snake-like (*hancha*) spiral. After baking, it is dusted with powdered sugar and criss-crossed with lines of ground cinnamon. It looks and tastes delicious and is quite easy to make.

INGREDIENTS

1 cup ground almonds	6 sheets filo pastry, 20 x 12 inches
1 tablespoon powdered sugar	flour and water paste
1 teaspoon powdered cinnamon	1 egg, beaten
1/4 cup orange-blossom water	powdered sugar
2 tablespoons clarified butter or butter, melted	powdered cinnamon

METHOD

■ To make the filling, mix together the almonds, sugar, and cinnamon, and then add the orange-blossom water and melted clarified butter or butter. Form into a paste of thick, moldable texture. You'll need to add a little water to achieve this, but be careful not to make it wet. Roll into 6 cylinder shapes slightly shorter than the length of the filo sheets.

■ Preheat the oven to 375°F, and have two damp, clean tea towels ready.

■ Open the filo package, take out 6 sheets and cover five with one of the towels. Spread the sixth sheet flat on a large, clean work surface, and place the first almond cylinder on to it. Roll the sheet up as tightly as you can, and cover with the second towel.

■ Spread the next sheet of filo out and place the next almond cylinder onto it. Run a smear of flour and water paste down one short edge. Overlap the first rolled-up pastry onto this pasted edge, then roll it up to make a double-length cylinder. Now curl this double cylinder into a tight spiral. Place on a greased round flan pan.

■ Repeat with the next two sheets and add them onto the spiral in the pan (overlap the seam so it won't show).

■ Repeat with the last two sheets and your spiral should now be 10 to 12 inches in diameter.

■ Glaze the coil with the beaten egg.

METHOD

■ Bake in the oven for 10 minutes. (It should be pale golden in color.) Remove and turn the spiral over. Bake another 10 minutes, or until it is the color gold of your choice (pale to dark).

■ Remove again. Turn the spiral back over again, and sprinkle with powdered sugar. Put it on a serving plate and carefully draw a grid of brown lines of cinnamon powder over the white sugar.

Curly Pastry Ribbons

RIGHAIF

MAKES 12
RIGHAIFS

If you are fortunate enough to visit a Moroccan pastry shop, you had better not be on a diet, because it will be full of temptation. *Righaif* are bound to be there, curly ribbons of pastry wound around into a circle about 3 inches in diameter. They are deep-fried to a golden brown, then laced with honey and sprinkled with sesame seeds.

A version is called *shebhakiah* using the same pastry but shaped into small flower-petal shapes.

INGREDIENTS

1 cup all-purpose flour	1/2 teaspoon salt
2 tablespoons fresh yeast	vegetable oil for deep-frying
2 teaspoons white sugar	1 cup honey
1 egg	1 tablespoon sesame seeds
3 tablespoons clarified butter or butter, melted	

METHOD

■ To make the pastry, sieve the flour into a large mixing bowl.

■ Dissolve the yeast in 1/2 cup warm water, then add the sugar.

■ Mix this into the flour with the egg, clarified butter or butter, salt, and just enough water to make a stiff dough.

■ Knead it well, then leave it to rest on a floured board. In a deep frying pan, heat the oil to 375°F. In a separate large, shallow pan, gently heat the honey.

■ Divide the dough into 4 equal pieces and shape each into a square.

■ Roll the first square out to a large, thin shape. Then using a curly pastry wheel, cut to a square with 10-inch sides. Cut the square into 6 strips.

METHOD

■ Pick up two strips, join them together, and curl them into an irregular circle. Immediately immerse this in the deep-frying oil and fry until golden, about 6 to 8 minutes.

■ Drain on paper towels, then immerse in the hot simmering honey for 10 seconds. Remove and sprinkle with sesame seeds.

■ While the first one is frying, repeat until there are 3 *righaifs* cooking together. Remove them in the order they went in.

■ Repeat until all 12 are cooked. They are normally served cold.

Fried Semolina Pudding

IRMIK HELVASI

SERVES 4

This Turkish pudding is much more delicious than its simple name suggests. It is quick to make, although a certain amount of stirring is required. In essence it is a stir-fry of the ingredients, cooked to a lovely pale brown color, and with a soft, paste-like texture. It can be served cold, but it is infinitely nicer hot. As a study of the ingredients shows, it is extremely rich, so small helpings are in order. Variations of this pudding are found all over the Middle East—and in India.

INGREDIENTS

1/2 cup butter	1/2 cup whipping cream
1/4 cup pine nuts	1/2 cup packed brown sugar
1 cup semolina	3 or 4 drops vanilla extract
1 cup milk	

METHOD

■ In a medium skillet, melt the butter over medium heat. Add the pine nuts and sauté for 2 minutes.

■ Add the semolina and continue to cook about 5 minutes until it becomes golden.

■ Add the milk, cream, sugar, and vanilla extract a little at a time in about 4 or 5 stages, stirring it until it thickens each time.

■ Serve hot or, if preferred, spread it on a flat baking sheet to cool. Cut into slices when cold.

Sweet Cheese Pancakes

BLINTZE

**MAKES 12 TO
14 PANCAKES**

These absolutely delicious Israeli cream cheese-filled pancakes are either served as a savory dish (with salt), or sweet, as in this recipe from the stunning Seven Arches restaurant in Jerusalem's Hotel Inter-Continental.

INGREDIENTS

1/2 cup all-purpose flour	1/2 cup thick sour cream
1/4 cup butter, melted, plus extra for frying	2 tablespoons brown sugar
2 eggs, beaten	1 teaspoon powdered cinnamon
1 cup warm milk	1 teaspoon ground green cardamom
1 tablespoon sugar	powdered sugar
3 or 4 drops vanilla extract	lemon wedges
1 cup curd cheese or labnah (see page 25)	

METHOD

■ To make the pancakes, sift the flour into a bowl and mix in the butter, eggs, milk, sugar, and vanilla. Combine thoroughly and let stand for about 10 minutes. The batter should be of pouring consistency.

■ To make the filling, mix together the cheese or labnah, sour cream, sugar, cinnamon, and cardamom in a bowl.

■ In a very hot omelette or griddle pan, heat a little butter. Pour in enough batter which, when swirled around the pan, makes a thin pancake.

■ Cook to set, then turn over and briefly cook the other side. Turn it out and place some of the filling across the center of the pancake.

■ Tuck in two sides, then roll it up to create a cylinder, and keep warm. Serve with a dusting of powdered sugar and a squeeze of lemon.

Syrupy Pancakes

ATAIF OR QATAAYIF

MAKES 12 TO 14 PANCAKES

All over the Arab Islamic world these pancakes make a symbolic and eagerly awaited appearance to mark the end of the month-long annual fast of Ramadan. They bear some resemblance to the pancakes traditionally eaten on Shrove Tuesday. They are served hot or cold, folded to a semicircle or rolled up, then drenched with hot syrup or honey and served with or without the thick Arab clotted cream (*kaymak*) and/or chopped nuts. There is also a savory version using a cream cheese filling mixed with herbs. This recipe is from Bahrain.

INGREDIENTS

PANCAKES AND FILLING

1 recipe blintze pancakes (see page 159)

1 cup chopped walnuts or other nuts

2 tablespoons brown sugar

1 teaspoon ground green cardamom

1/2 teaspoon grated nutmeg

SYRUP ('ATARI) AND GARNISH

1/2 cup maple syrup

1/4 cup honey

2 tablespoons lemon juice

orange-blossom water

rose water

minced pistachio nuts

METHOD

■ Follow the recipe for blintzes to the stage just prior to filling.

■ Fold each pancake in half and pinch the edges together. Set aside and keep warm.

■ To make the syrup, heat the maple syrup, honey, and lemon juice in a small saucepan. Drench the pancakes with the syrup.

■ Sprinkle with orange-blossom water, rose water and pistachio nuts, and serve piping hot.

Ali's Mom's Pudding

UM M'ALI

SERVES 4

Probably the best description of this thrifty dish is bread and butter pudding, Middle Eastern style. This particular version is from Egypt, and it uses scraps of dried filo pastry. The Egyptians also use a type of cracker called *raqaq*, which is sold in packets. Khoubiz and other bread can also be used.

I have seen some pretty bizarre explanations of the name of this pudding, including an Irish connection (that it was the invention of one Mrs. O'Malley, which has to be pure blarney!). *Um* (or *om*) in Arabic means "mother" and Ali is as common a name as John. So the most likely literal translation is Ali's mom.

INGREDIENTS

10 to 12 ounces filo or khoubiz bread	10 to 12 whole cloves
vegetable oil for deep-frying	1 teaspoon powdered cinnamon
1/4 cup pine nuts	1 teaspoon ground green cardamom
1/2 cup walnuts, almonds, or pistachio nuts, chopped (or a combination)	2 16-ounce cans sweetened condensed milk
1/4 cup sultanas or raisins	1/2 cup milk or cream
1/4 cup dates, pitted and chopped	

METHOD

■ Preheat the oven to 400°F. In a deep frying pan, deep-fry the pieces of filo or bread. Drain on paper towels, cool, and break into small pieces.

■ Spread the pieces on the base of a 10- x 8-inch baking dish.

■ Cover with the nuts, sultanas or raisins, dates, cloves, cinnamon, and cardamom.

■ Warm (don't boil) the two milks together until they thicken. Then pour into the baking dish, making sure that the other ingredients are completely covered.

■ Bake for 15 to 20 minutes, until the top forms a golden crust. Serve hot.

Stuffed Dates

SEPHARDI TAMAR

SERVES 4 TO 6

Dates are synonymous with the Middle East, the date palm evoking images of deserts and oases. Dates grow profusely, just about everywhere, especially in Algeria, Tunisia, Iran, and Israel. There are over 300 varieties and they range in color from gold to red and dark brown. Two of the best varieties are *deglet noor* and *medjool*.

Dates are eaten fresh, used in cooking, and they are preserved (as we know them best, a Christmas delicacy in those fancy gift boxes). In the Middle East they are eaten year-round, at any meal, unaccompanied, with yogurt, or stuffed with savory or sweet fillings. In this particularly succulent Israeli recipe they make an excellent dessert.

INGREDIENTS

1 1/2 cups packed preserved dates or 16 to 20 fresh ripe dates	1 tablespoon sugar
2 tablespoons ground almonds	1 teaspoon minced pistachio nuts
1/4 cup butter, softened	1 quantity syrup ('atari) (see page 160).

METHOD

▪ Carefully slit the dates down one side and remove the pits.

▪ To make the filling, mix the almonds, butter, sugar, and pistachio nuts in a bowl. Add a little water to achieve a marzipan texture, then shape into pieces the size of the date pits.

▪ Insert the filling into the dates.

▪ Make the syrup following the recipe on page 160. (Any extra filling can be put in the syrup, or it can be frozen for future use.)

▪ Arrange the dates on a serving dish, and pour the hot syrup over them. Chill before serving.

Turkish Delight

RAHAT LOKUM

**MAKES ABOUT
32 PIECES**

Nothing has probably done more to promote a particular image of Turkey than this sweet—opulence, wealth, harems, voluptuous belly-dancers, and overweight sultans. It is an image which has nothing whatsoever to do with modern Turkey but it endures, as does Turkish Delight.

It can be made at home, but it is a recipe which needs patience and care to get it from a liquid to a gelatinous texture. The traditional ingredient for thickening is mastic, but you can use gelatin. Some recipes use cornflour, but this makes for a rather heavier texture. Many recipes require 2 to 3 hours of continuous stirring, but the following is, by those standards, quick and effort-free.

INGREDIENTS

1 1/4 cups water, divided	1/4 cup water
2 cups white sugar	1/2 teaspoon rose water
2 teaspoons lemon juice	melted butter
1/8 teaspoon red food coloring (optional)	powdered sugar
2 tablespoons powdered gelatin	

METHOD

■ Bring 1 cup of the water to a boil in a heavy saucepan, then add the sugar, lemon juice, and coloring, if desired. Combine thoroughly.

■ Continue to boil for 10 to 15 minutes. As it thickens, continue to stir until it is reduced to a thick but easily pourable syrup. Remove from the heat and set aside to cool for 10 minutes.

■ Dissolve the gelatin in the remaining water. Add it to the syrup, stir in well, and bring it to a simmer. Add the rose water.

■ Select a small baking pan such as a round tart pan about 6 1/2 inches in diameter and 1 1/2 inches deep. Brush with melted butter.

■ Pour the syrup into the pan and refrigerate for 24 hours.

■ It should be firmly set like a jelly. Turn it out onto a board and sprinkle with powdered sugar. Cut into 1-inch-square pieces. Store in an airtight container where they will keep for a few weeks.

Note: Alternatives include the addition of green food coloring in place of red, and hopped pistachio nuts added at the same time as the rose water. Or omit food coloring and rose water and add 1 teaspoon of vanilla extract.

163

Sugared Almonds

LOSE HILOO

SERVES 4

These whole almonds, fried in butter and dusted in sugar, are delicious served cold as a garnish to sweet dishes or on their own with coffee or tea. They are simplicity itself to make and any nuts can be used this way.

INGREDIENTS

1/4 cup butter	powdered sugar
1 cup shelled whole almonds	

METHOD

- Melt the butter in a frying pan.

- Add the almonds and sauté for 2 to 3 minutes, turning them frequently.

- Strain off the butter and set aside.

- Allow the almonds to cool, then dust with the sugar.

- Store in an airtight container where they will keep for months.

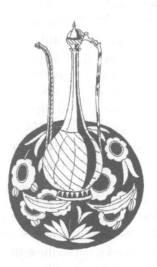

AFTER THE MEAL

▲▲▲▲▲▲▲▲▲▲▲▲▲▲▲▲▲

In a culture where alcohol is either forbidden, severely disapproved of, or barely tolerated, other beverages have taken its place. They always appear after the meal, and endlessly throughout the day.

COFFEE

In many Middle Eastern countries, coffee is the favored brew. Traditionally it is very strong and thick, with a layer of sludge at the bottom.

Coffee is now a worldwide phenomenon, but it was the Arabs who discovered it growing wild in Abyssinia (now Ethiopia), the African country across the narrow waters of the Red Sea from Saudi Arabia. Roots and berries had been infused in boiling water since ancient times to produce hot brews, so it is not surprising that coffee beans were eventually subjected to this process. Exactly when this first took place and how the process of roasting raw green beans before grinding and brewing them was conceived, is not known. The Arabs imported Abyssinian coffee into the ancient Yemeni port of Al Mukha. Most researchers agree that coffee was being cultivated in the area by A.D. 550, 100 years before Islam. The harvest was small, and the brew confined to a few devotees. That coffee was a powerful stimulant was recognized by the early fanatical followers of Mohammed, who regarded it almost as unfavorably as they did alcohol. But it escaped prohibition, and indeed it was later generations of Moslem monks, the dervishes, who made coffee drinking ritualistic, significant, and permanent.

Despite the rapid spread of Arab power over the next few centuries, coffee drinking was unknown outside southern Arabia. This was possibly because of the importance it had achieved in Islamic religious ceremony, particularly in Mecca. There it must have been tasted by Moslem pilgrims who flocked to Mecca from all parts of the vast Islamic world to pay homage to Mohammed. But it took 1,000 years for coffee to become known to the world outside Arabia. With the shift of the balance of power to Turkey in the fifteenth century, it was inevitable that coffee would follow. The honors of introducing the infusion to the Ottoman court fell, it is said, to a Syrian spice merchant. The Arab *q'ahwah* became the Turkish *khave*. It became imme-diately popular all over the Ottoman Empire, and within a century it was widely consumed from North Africa to Armenia. Its introduction to Europe was equally spectacular. The Christian church was at first as suspicious of coffee as the early Moslems and it took a papal edict for it to be accepted.

It was the Turkish ambassador to France who created a sensation in 1669, when he offered coffee to his guests, thereby introducing coffee to Europe for the first time. And it was an Armenian who just three years later opened the first coffee shop in Paris. Within a decade coffee shops were opened in every fashionable European city. Business was conducted in them and they became the forerunners of banks, finance houses, and gentlemen's clubs. Coffee reached the New World during the eighteenth century, and most of the world's coffee now comes from South America.

Arab and Turkish coffees are identical in preparation. The traditional bean is the *mocha* (named after the port of Al Mukha). This is a dark, strong, full-bodied coffee, ground to a very fine powder. Households all over the Middle East have coffee all during their waking hours. Its serving remains as much a ritual as it was hundreds of years ago. Now it is one of hospitality rather than of religion.

The ritual begins with the roasting, cooling, and pulverizing of the coffee bean—it must be done freshly either at home or by a coffee merchant in a *tahrini* (coffee grinder). It is brewed in a brass or enameled pot made for the purpose, a vessel with a narrow neck and long handle which holds between one and six servings of coffee. The cups themselves are tiny, smaller than demitasse measures, with or without handles. In formal situations, at table, for example, the coffee is poured by the host, the first cup is passed to the senior guest, then the remaining cups are passed round the table anticlockwise. The host refills the cups in the order they were served until the drinkers indicate by a wiggle of the cup that they have had enough.

The first time a Westerner has this kind of coffee it can come as a surprise. It is always taken black and the coffee powder is not filtered into the cup. The result is that about one-third of the liquid is a totally unpalatable sludge which settles on the bottom of the cup. One therefore sips only the top half of one's cup, which in reality is only a mouthful or two. For this reason one is expected to drink two or three cups. To drink less is an insult to the host (but to drink more will keep you awake all night, it is very strong indeed!). It is also normally brewed with a lot of sugar, although the sweetness index can be to the drinker's taste—*ziyadda* or *hilou* is extra sweet, *mazboutah* or *madhbout* is just a little sugar, and *murrah* is without sugar. Sugarless coffee symbol-izes times of unhappiness—it is taken for example by all participants at a funeral.

Coffee Western-style is now becoming almost as popular in the Arab world as the traditional coffee. The term *q'ahwah Fransawi* (literally French coffee) covers everything from filtered grounds to instant coffee.

Arab Coffee

Q'AHWAH ARABIYA

This is the original Middle Eastern infusion brewed with the aromatic flavor of cardamom.

METHOD

■ The strength of the brew is up to you, but it is normally 2 teaspoons per cup for strong, and 1 teaspoon for medium. Add sugar to taste in the ratio of 1 teaspoon per cup sweet, 1/2 teaspoon medium sweet, and so on. Finally, add ground green cardamom, 1/2 teaspoon per cup. Mix all these ingredients.

■ Into a saucepan, measure the exact quantity of water you intend to drink in one of the cups you will use (6 full measures for 6 cups), and bring to a boil.

■ Add the ingredients mentioned in the first step, and bring back to a boil. Simmer for about 10 minutes.

■ Return to a boil, and serve at once to ensure that each cup gets a similar amount of grounds.

■ Allow 1 or 2 minutes for the grounds to settle before drinking.

Yemeni Coffee

Q'SHR

Prepare exactly as for Arabic coffee, but use 1/4 teaspoon of ground ginger per cup in place of the cardamom.

Turkish Coffee

KHAVE TURKI

This is the coffee many of us will be familiar with from Turkish restaurants (in Greek restaurants it is called Greek coffee!). Spices are omitted, and the brewing method is lighter, creating a topping of foam.

METHOD

- Use the same measures of ground Turkish coffee to determine strength. Sugar strengths are the same too, but the Turkish terms are *sekerli*, very sweet, *orta*, medium sweet, and *sade*, sugarless.

- Put the measured water into a pan along with the coffee and sugar.

- Bring to a boil until it froths. Take the pan off the heat, and allow to cool for just a minute.

- Repeat the last instruction twice more then serve the coffee immediately to ensure that each cup gets an equal amount of grounds. Try to pour a little froth *(wijih)* into each cup.

- Allow the grounds to settle in the cup for a minute or two before drinking.

Maghreb Coffee

Q'AHWEH M'GREBI

Follow either the Arab or Turkish method. In place of cardamom, add 1/4 teaspoon powdered cinnamon. Just before serving add 1 drop orange-blossom water per person.

Tea

In some Middle Eastern countries tea is drunk much more than coffee, especially in Iran, Armenia, and surprisingly, perhaps, Turkey. Despite their imagined predilection for coffee, tea drinking in Turkey far outweighs that of coffee as it does in the Maghreb, where the delectable *chai bi na'na*, or mint tea, is universally enjoyed.

Moroccan Mint Tea

CHAI BI NA'NA

SERVES 4

The Berbers have been drinking an infusion with fresh mint since they first inhabited the Maghreb thousands of years ago. It took the British to make the only significant change the brew had known in its long life. After the start of the Crimean War, many of the British tea traders' central European markets disappeared overnight. Desperate to sell their surplus tea the traders tried, amongst other places, North Africa. They discovered the mint brew and suggested that tea be added to it, and it became an instant success. It is a wonderfully refreshing drink—especially on a summer's afternoon. The teas that blend most sympathetically with mint are green Chinese teas such as oolong, jasmine, or green gunpowder. Spearmint is the mint widely used to make Moroccan tea, but other varieties, especially peppermint, are equally interesting (see Herbs Glossary).

INGREDIENTS

3 cups water	4 fresh mint sprigs
3 to 4 teaspoons tea leaves	sugar lumps to taste
20 to 30 spearmint leaves	

METHOD

- Boil the water in a kettle.

- Warm the teapot. Put the tea and mint leaves in and add the boiling water.

- Leave it to brew for 2 or 3 minutes.

- While the teas is brewing, warm tumblers by rinsing in hot water.

- Put one sprig of mint into each tumbler.

- Pour the tea into each tumbler through a strainer. It is normal to add sugar lumps to the teapot, but it can be added to the tumbler to taste after pouring.

169

Armenian Tea

HAIGANAN TEY

SERVES 4

Cinnamon is used in this Caucasian tea to produce a sweet, very fragrant infusion. Made with or without tea leaves, this recipe uses cinnamon and a delicate smoky tea such as Chinese keemun, lapsang souchong, or fan yong. No milk is used.

INGREDIENTS

3 cups water	3 to 4 teaspoons tea leaves
6 cloves	sugar to taste
4 2 1/2-inch cinnamon sticks	

METHOD

- Follow the mint tea recipe on page 169 through the brewing instructions, using cloves and cinnamon instead of the mint.

- Pour the tea into a tumbler through a strainer. Sweeten to taste.

Turkish Tea

CHAIY TURKI

SERVES 4

Tea drinking probably arrived in Turkey at the time of the Ottomans, over 400 years ago. Their tea was imported from Persia until plantations were established in the Black Sea area under British supervision about 100 years ago. Contrary to popular supposition, much more tea is drunk in Turkey than coffee. It is always on hand in special teapots and is served without milk in special small tumblers.

Turkish tea is sometimes obtainable in the West. Otherwise use any tea of your choice—Assam from India will, for example, give a strong reddish brew, while jasmine tea from China is very delicately scented with jasmine blossoms.

INGREDIENTS

3 cups water	4 to 6 teaspoons tea leaves

METHOD

- Follow the recipe for mint tea on page 169 through the brewing process. Omit the mint.

170

GLOSSARIES

This section is subdivided into herb and spice sections followed by a general glossary. The purpose of the general glossary is to enable the user to identify the Middle Eastern ingredients, techniques, and terms used in this book. All words are Arabic or English unless otherwise stated.

HERB GLOSSARY
(see also page 18)

Basil (rayhan, reeyan)
Large flat green leaf
A most fragrant and delightful herb, easily obtainable in the West.

Chervil
Delicate feathery leaf
A native to the area, it has a parsley/aniseed flavor. Used as a garnish.

Coriander (kazbara, kuzbarah)
Flat green leaf
Widely used in Middle Eastern cooking. The leaves are called kuzbarah khadra (fresh coriander) to distinguish them from the seeds (see Spice Glossary). Named after the Greek word "korus," a bedbug, apparently because the leaf's slightly fetid smell resembles these pests.

Cress (barbeen)
Dark green leaf
Of the mustard family. Resembles watercress but with much smaller leaves. Used in Iranian stews where it is called shahat, and all over the Gulf, both in cooking and salads. There are many other varieties of cress. Jargeer is sharp tasting.

Dill (shabth)
Feathery blue-green leaf
An ideal garnish, its aniseed flavor also enhances meat, vegetable, or rice dishes.

Fennel (shummar)
Feathery, green leaf
Used as dill.

Garlic Chives (tareh)
Flat-bladed leaf
Native to and used in Iranian cooking. Its leaves are larger than ordinary chives, but it has, as its name states, a garlicky taste. Also called Chinese chives.

Marjoram (samaq itrah)
Sweet-scented flower, small leaves
Powerful aroma but easily lost if overcooked. It is usually added fresh to the dish a couple of minutes before serving.

171

Marjoram, Wild (rigani)
Bitter-sweet flower and small leaves

Related to marjoram, there are several varieties. Used in Greek cooking to flavor items such as kebabs. It is difficult to obtain in the West.

Melokhia
Spinach-like darkish green leaf

Member of the jute family, virtually exclusive to Egypt, and rarely found fresh elsewhere. The dried variety lacks flavor. The Egyptians use it to flavor many savory dishes. Its most celebrated Egyptian use is in one of the country's national dishes—the soup called appropriately melokhia.

Mint (na'na)
Bright green leaf

Various varieties grow everywhere. The most common type to be used in cooking is spearmint. Always best fresh, it is used in a variety of ways: stewed in the mint tea of Morocco (see page 169), fried and added to Arab soups, dried in stews and chutneys, and fresh in salads. It is one of the most distinctive tastes of the Middle East. Na'na literally means "the gift of Allah."

Parsley (bagdunis)
Flat green leaf

In the Middle East, most parsley is flat-leaved rather than the Western curly-leaved variety but they taste the same.

Purslane (bakli, baglah, farfhin)
Green, fleshy leaf growing on red stalk

Spinach-like vegetable which grows in the wild and is also cultivated. Particularly popular in the Levant, where it is notable in fatoush, a fresh salad containing toasted bread. It used to be popular in Elizabethan England in stews, but is hard to come by in the West today.

Rosemary (hasa il-ban or iklil bi jabal)
Silvery-grey spiky tough leaf

Particularly popular in Morocco (where it appears in ras-el-hanout). A very aromatic, distinctive herb.

Sage (maramiyah)
Oblong green leaf

Popular in kebab marinades and in salads, sage is fairly powerful and should be used sparingly.

Thyme (za'atar)
Small grey-green leaf

Widely used as a background flavor in casseroles, this too is a powerful herb.

SPICE GLOSSARY
(see also page 18)

Allspice (bahar hah hilu)
Round dark brown seeds

The allspice seed looks like a large peppercorn. It fooled its discoverer, Christopher Columbus, who located it in Jamaica and named it pimento or Jamaican pepper. The confusion remains to this day. It is not a member of the pepper family and "allspice" describes it better. Its taste is quite aromatic, resembling a combination of cinnamon, clove, ginger, nutmeg, and pepper itself. This conveniently packages in one item the flavor enjoyed all over the Middle East, and it is therefore widely used there.

Aniseed (yansoon)
Small grey-green seeds

Native to the area. One of the first spices to be cultivated in Egypt. It appears in savory and sweet dishes and is fundamental to the spirits ouzo and raki. Its main essential oil is anethole, also present in the nonrelated fennel and star anise.

Barberry (zereshk)
Red-brown berries

The berries are dried whole and resemble currants in texture and color but not in taste. They are very sour, and are used whole in Iranian cooking.

Bay Leaves (waraq il ghar)
Green spear-shaped leaves

Native to Asia Minor. Used in the same way as in the West to flavor stews, etc., fresh or dried, especially in Greece and Turkey.

Caraway (karawya)
Small, thin, black seeds

Has been used for over 5,000 years as a cooking spice, in pastries, savories, sweets, and salads.

Cardamom, Green (hayl or hab han)
Green pod cases containing aromatic black seeds

Native to India and brought back by the Middle Eastern traders in the centuries B.C., it is an expensive spice, but is widely used, especially in Arabia and Iran to flavor Arab coffee.

Cassia (darseen) and Cinnamon (kirfee)
Brown bark pieces or quills

The inner bark of evergreen trees closely related but from different species. Both are used for the sweetness the bark imparts. Cassia is native to China, is cheaper and generally more robust. Cinnamon is native to Sri Lanka, and was taken to China and later traded to the Middle East.

Chile (bisbas, fel fel or filfil)
Fleshy green pods

Members of the capsicum family, which turn red when ripe. There are over 1,500 species ranging in size from tiny to very large and in heat grading from mild to volcanic. Native to Latin America, they were not introduced to the Arab lands until the sixteenth century. Until then Indian pepper was the primary heat source in cooking. They are now a part of the way of life in some countries.

Clove (habahan, kabsh kurnful)
Dark brown "nail"-shaped (from the Latin "clavus" meaning nail)

The rounded "head" of the clove is an unopened flower bud. Cropping is slow and expensive, and if mistimed and the flower opens, the clove is useless. Native to the Moluccan Islands in Indonesia (although few grow there now), they were a major trading crop in medieval times. Today they are mainly harvested in Zanzibar, Madagascar, and Grenada. One of the few spices to have remained in constant use in Britain, both in cooking (apples for example) and medicine (the oil is a soother at the dentist). They have a widespread application in Middle Eastern cooking.

Coriander (kazbara)
Round pale brown seeds (see also page 171)
The seeds of the coriander plant are infrequently used whole in Middle Eastern cooking, but ground, they are used in many recipes. They impart a sweetish, slightly musky taste, quite unlike fresh coriander leaves.

Cumin (kammun)
Small greenish seeds

Native to upper Egypt and the Levant, cumin has been found in the Pyramids. One of the most popular spices, especially so in Morocco and Tunisia, where it is the only spice used in some dishes.

Cumin, Black (habet el baraka)
Small, thin, black seeds

In appearance similar to caraway with which they are often confused, but their taste is much less sweet and more astringent. Used in rice dishes.

Fenugreek (hilbah, hulba)
Golden brown nugget-like seeds
An Asian native, long since brought to the West, the name derives from the Latin "*fenum graecum*," or Greek leaves. It is, however, scarcely used in Greek cooking, and that derivation probably refers to the time when the Greek empire extended as far as India,

where the seed and its leaves are an important curry ingredient. Fenugreek is powerful, and an acquired taste, being bitter when raw, but less so when cooked. It is not universally popular in the Middle East. Iranian cooking uses both seed and leaf, and the Iraqis use the seed in certain dishes. One specialty that does use it is *pastourma*, dried salt beef. It is ground into a paste and rubbed onto the beef prior to drying. This same dish is found in Turkey and Armenia (*aboukht*). In the Yemen, the specialty *hilbeh*, named after the spice itself, is a very hot dip containing fenugreek and coriander (see page 36). It is also baked in bread (see page 146).

Ginger (zanjabil)
Irregularly shaped root covered with dry, parchment-colored skin

This rhizome, native to the South East Asian jungle, is now grown in India and many other tropical countries. The fresh root travels well, keeps for months, and is now well known in the grocery stores of the West. Dry or powdered ginger can be used as a substitute, and it was this form that the Arabs first traded with Chinese merchants. It is, in fact, not used extensively in Middle Eastern cooking.

Mahlab
Mahlab has no English translation and is only found in the Middle East. The spice is obtained from the seed of a black cherry originally native to Syria. The seed is opened and discarded after the kernel, a pale brown seed the size of a peppercorn, the *mahlab* itself, is extracted. It is always sold whole and must be freshly ground to retain its sweet, aromatic properties and it is only used in baking. The Arab bun *ka'ak* or the Armenian *choerig* biscuit, and other cakes and breads containing *mahlab*, have a unique flavor.

Nutmeg (jawaz a'tib)
Hard, round, pale, brown ball

Native to South East Asia, it was introduced to the West by the earliest Arab and Chinese traders. It is a kernel around which the lattice-like mace grows, the outer case being a pithy green fruit. Nutmeg is widely used in the Middle East, especially in the spice mix *baharat*.

Paprika (filfil hilu)
Bright red ground pepper

Made from red capsicum bell peppers, the Arabic meaning literally "peppersweet." It is used for coloring as much as flavoring.

Pepper, Black (filfil aswan)
Whole black corns or ground

An important spice, well-known worldwide.

Pepper, White (filfil beida)
Whole white corns or ground

As well known as black pepper.

Pomegranate (ruman, anar)
Deep reddish-brown sticky seeds

Native to Iran and much relished there. The soft round fruit is eaten raw with salt or sugar. Both flesh and seeds are used in Iranian cooking as a souring agent. In the Levant, the seeds, fresh or dried, are compressed to produce a dark brown syrup (grenadine) used for flavoring foods, or, with plentiful sugar, as a drink (especially favored in the Gulf). The dry seeds are also used as a garnish. Pomegranate has always been greatly respected. Genesis claims it to be the tree of life (it was more than likely the apple in the garden of Eden), and the Koran states that the consumption of pomegranate represses thoughts of envy. At the Turkish wedding ceremony, a custom from ancient times is to throw a whole ripe pomegranate to the ground. The number of seeds spilling out tells how many children the couple will have.

Poppy Seed
Tiny blue or cream-colored seeds

There are many species of poppy, including the opium varieties. Poppy seeds contain no opium. The blue or cream seeds are from different species, but the taste is the same. They are primarily used to garnish bread and cakes. On the Jewish holiday Purim, a triangular pastry, *hamantaschen*, containing poppy seeds is the specialty of the day. The Egyptians at the times of the Pharaohs favored poppy seeds, and the Greeks fed their Olympic athletes on honey and poppy seed cakes.

Saffron (za'faran)
Deep orange/crimson threads

The threads are the stigma of a particular species of crocus. Three grow in each crocus and they must be gently hand-picked at exactly the right moment of ripeness, then dried as soon as possible. The method of cropping cannot be automated and this, coupled with the fact that it takes 225,000 stigmas, or 75,000 crocuses to make 1 lb (450 g) of saffron, makes it the world's most expensive spice. It originated in Turkey, and now is grown in Iran, Kashmir, and Spain, where the Arabs planted it in the tenth century. The very word saffron is derived from the Arabic *za'faran* meaning yellow, and it is as a fragrant colorer that it is mostly used. Although it is used in dishes involving prolonged cooking, it is wasted in this role—all its flavor is lost.

Sesame (sum sum)
Small, flat, round, pale cream seeds

These come in other colors, including red, brown, and black, the latter being used in Chinese cooking. But it is the cream seed (called white) which is so widely used in the Middle East, where it is indigenous. Today it is pressed into an oil, included in baking, but its most widespread use is in the mixture tahini.

Sumak (sumaq)
Dried very dark red berries

The berries from the *sumaq* tree, native to Iran, are used whole or ground as a souring agent in cooking in all sorts of meat or vegetable dishes. It is also used in fish dishes, which can lead to confusion, as the Arabic word for fish is *samak* (singular) and *sameq* (plural), and the dish *sameq al harrah* is fish baked with chile, tahini, garlic, pine nuts and *sumaq*.

Turmeric (kurkum)
Fine yellow powder

Native to South Asia, turmeric is a rhizome which, like ginger, can be cooked fresh. Turmeric is normally encountered ground, though, and is used primarily for giving color. It is bitter, so is used sparingly, and although recipe books claim it can be substituted for saffron, it will give neither the brightness and individuality of color nor the fragrance of saffron. Turmeric is widely used in Indian curry (the Arabic *kurkum* could be another derivative of the word "curry"). In the Middle East it is used in countries as far apart as Morocco and Iran.

GENERAL GLOSSARY

A

Aadou—Mezzeh (Tunisia)
Aash—Iranian soup (Persian)
Abgusht—Meat cooked with yogurt and spices (Persian)
Ads—Lentils
Ageen—Pastry
Aish or Aiysh—Bread (Egyptian)
Ajja—Omelette
Anar—Pomegranate
Arak—Alcoholic beverage made from grape flavored with aniseed. Widely enjoyed where Moslem laws do not apply. Called raki in Turkey, oghi in Armenia, ouzo in Greece
Arnhab—Rabbit
Assafeer—Quail
Assal—Honey
Atari—Syrup

B

Bagdunis—Parsley
Bahar—Mixture of four spices (clove, cinnamon, nutmeg, and pepper)
Bahar Hah Hilu—Allspice
Baharat or Bharat—The above mixture, plus coriander, cumin, pepper, and paprika
Baidh—Egg
Balch or Baglah—Purslane
Bamia—Okra
Bamir—Cheese made from milk curds (Armenian) similar to Indian panir and Turkish peynir. Usually milk of sheep or cow, occasionally goat or mare.
Barbeen—Cress
Basal—Onion
Basterma—Spicy dried beef (Armenia)
Bataresh—Salty Egyptian fish roe
Batellu—Veal
Batt—Duck

Bekmez—Thick grape juice syrup
Berenje—Rice (Iran)
Bhar—See Bahar
Bisbas—Chile
Booza-booza—Ice cream
Borani—Iranian salad with yogurt
Bulgur—Wheat is husked, partly cooked, dried, then ground to three grades—coarse for stuffing and rice dishes, medium for fillings, and fine for salads. Bulgur originated with the earliest civilizations in the Levant and was probably mankind's first processed food.

C

Couscous—Semolina product
Couscousière—Couscous cooking pot

D

Dajaj—Chicken
Damassa—Egyptian utensil for cooking ful (beans)
Danee—Lamb
Darseen—Cassia
Dersa—Hot, spicy Algerian sauce
Dibbis Rhumas or Dibs Romana—Syrup made from pomegranate used to flavor savory dishes (Lebanese)
Djej—Chicken
Dolma—Stuffed vegetable (Turkish), dolmades (Greek), dolmeh (Persian)
Doner—Type of kebab found all over the Middle East but originating in Turkey
Dukkah—Dry spice/nut/herb mixtures

E

Eggah—Omelette (Egyptian)

F

Fakhid—Leg (of lamb)
Farfhin—Purslane
Fel Fel—Chile
Fel Fel Sudani—Hot spicy sauce from Morocco
Falafel—Chickpea croquette
Ferakh—Chicken
Ferakh Hadjal—Partridge
Feta—Goat cheese found in Greece, Turkey, and Iran
Filfil Ahmar—Chile pepper, red
Filfil Aswah—Black pepper
Filfil Beida—White pepper
Filfil Hilu—Paprika
Filo, also Fila, Phila, Phyllo and Yufka—Very thinly rolled Greek pastry (see page ¨)
Firinda—Baked (Turkish)
Firri—Baby chicken or poussin
Ful—Broad beans (Egypt)
Ful Medamis—Small, round, brown beans, used to make the Egyptian "national dish"
Ful Nabed—Large, flat, round, broad beans with a pale brown skin. The actual beans are white and are used in bassarah and ta'amiah (Egyptian)

G

Gamar id-Din—Paste of cooked apricot. When used to make a drink it is called sharab gamar id-din
Gambari—Shrimps/prawns
Gamil—Camel
Girfar—Cinnamon
Gul Suyu—Rose water (Turkish)
Guvech—Cooking style where ingredients are baked in and eaten from a pottery dish (Turkish/Armenian)

H

Habahan—Clove
Hab Han—Green cardamom
Hab Hilu—Allspice
Habash—Turkey
Habb—Husked wheat kernels
Habet el Baraka—Black cumin
Halal—Moslem food preparation laws (see pages 10 and 64)
Halawal or Halva—A sweet or dessert
Haleeb—Milk
Haloumi—Salty cheese usually from milk, goat or sheep, sometimes cow (Lebanese), Hallumi (Greek), hellim (Turkish)
Hamaan—Pigeon
Hamindas—Eggs cooked in Israeli cholent (stew). Hamine similar in Egypt
Hasa il-Ban—Rosemary
Hayl—Green cardamom
Heloo or Hilu—Sweet
Hilba or Hilbeh or Hulba—Spice dip
Hummus—Chickpea (garbanzo bean), first cultivated in Egypt
Hout—Fish (Maghreb)
Humir—Tamarind
Huwmara—White flour

I

Iggah—Omelette
Istakoz—Lobster (Turkish)
Iklil bi Jabal—Rosemary

J

Jawaz a 'Tib—Nutmeg

K

Kabsh Kurnful—Cloves

Kammun—Cumin

Kandouz—Beef

Karawya—Caraway

Kazbara—Coriander

K'dra—Cooking with fat or samneh (Moroccan), see Mqali

Kebab or Kabab, Kabaub, Kobob—Literally means cooked meat. The Turks perfected marination and other methods. Doner means to turn, and shish, sis, sheesh, sheik means skewer in Turkish. Shashlik means meat and vegetables on a skewer (Armenian), hasina is the same thing in Persian, and shami is a ground meat cassrole (Syrian)

Kemia—Mezzeh (Algeria)

Khal—Vinegar

Kharouf—Lamb

Kharub—Carob. Pods of an evergreen tree dried in the sun, then enjoyed for their chocolate taste. Available in powdered form.

Khdar or Akhdar—Green

Khadra—Fresh

Khashkar—Brown flour

Khoubiz or Khobz, etc.—Standard Arabian bread

Khozi—Pork

Khudar—Vegetables

Khulinjan—Galingale

Kibbeh or Kibbi—Vegetables stuffed with a mixture of bulgur and meat

Kirfee—Cinnamon

Kiymeh—Minced (meat)

Kofta or Kofteh—Meatballs (Iranian)

Kosher—Jewish food preparation laws (see pages 3, 10 and 64)

Kunafeh—Shredded filo dough for making kadayif (see page 155)

Kurfee—Cinnamon

Kurkum—Turmeric

Kuzbarah—Coriander

L

La Kama—Spice mix (Moroccan)

Laban—Yogurt

Labnah—Cheesy yogurt

Laham—Meat

Laham Meshwi—Cooked meat

Lawz—Almonds

Limu Omani or Loorni or Noomi—Dried whole limes, or ground limes used to give sour taste to savory dishes (Iranian).

Loze—Almonds

M

Magli—Boiled

Mahlab—A spice

M'ahmar—Red

M'ali—Fried

Mansaaf—Bedouin banquet dish involving a whole roast lamb and rice. The eyes are regarded as the main delicacy.

Maramiyah—Sage

M'ashi(ya) or Mahchi—Stuffed

Masgeof—To grill or broil

Mashwi—All types of meat

Matbook—Cooked

Maward—Rose water (Arabic)

Mazaher—Orange blossoms distilled in water. Used in delicate meat and rice dishes, sweets and in coffee.

Mechoui or M'choui—To grill (Arabic), grill whole sheep (Maghreb)

Meffened or M'fenned—A topping (see Chapter Four)

Megli—Fried

Mehammer—Fried

Mekah—Pickled items in vinegar

Melokhia—Green plant shoots, a bit spinach-like, used in Egyptian dishes

Mergez or Mergues, Merguvez—Hot, spicy, dry sausage made from mutton or goat and flavored with harissa (Tunisian/Algerian)

Meshwi—All types of meat

Mezzeh—Mixed hors-d'oeuvres

Mikhatel—Pickled items in vinegar

Mishi—Stuffed

Mishmish or Mechmach—Apricot. Eaten fresh, ripe, and juicy, of course, but it makes other appearances. Dried, it is one of the sweet-sour agencies in Iranian meat dishes. It is also made into a paste which is used in cookery or to make drinks. During Ramadan many people drink sharab gamar-id-din made from this paste to break the fast.

Mishshi—Stuffed vegetables (see Kibbeh)

Mishwi—All types of meat

Missabek—Stewed

Mistika—Mastic. Edible resin (sap) from an evergreen shrub used especially in meat dishes to enhance flavors and to bind meat in kebabs

Mqali—Cooking with olive oil (Moroccan), see k'dra

Mqali—Pickled items in vinegar

Mugaddra—Lentils

Muhammer—Sweet rice

Mussir—Wild garlic

N

Na'na—Mint

Noomi—See Limu Omani

P

Pastrouma—Spicy dried beef (Israeli)

Peynir—See Bamir

Pilich—Chicken (Turkish)

Pita—The well-known unleavened bread with a pocket

Plaki—Cooking style. Fish or vegetable cooked in olive oil with herbs, tomato, and garlic. It originated in Byzantine times and is still eaten in Greece, Turkey, and Armenia

Pourgouri—See Bourgouri

Q

Qali—Vinegar

R

Raki—See Arak

Ras el Hanout—Celebrated Moroccan spice mix

Rayhan or Reeyan—Basil

Reuchta—Noodles. The word means "thread" in Persian and Arabic. Found in the Maghreb, there are two styles—jda (very thin) and noissara (1/2 inch squares)

Rghaif—Pancake dough (Maghreb)

Rigani—Type of wild marjoram

Ruman—Pomegranate

S

Sabzi—Vegetables or herbs (Iranian)

Samneh or Smen—Clarified butter

Samak—Fish

Samaq Itrah—Marjoram

Sbar—Spiced with tamarind

Shabth—Dill

Shorba—Soup

Shummar—Fennel

Smen—Clarified butter

Snawbar or Snorbeh—Pine nuts

Soudjuk—Dried sausage

Soumanate—Quail

Summak—Dried berries

Sum Sum—Sesame

Susmeyagli—See *Smen*

T

Ta'amiah—Football-shaped croquette made from ful nabed beans. The Egyptian version of falafel.

Tagine—Type of slow-cooked stew (Moroccan)

Tahini or Tahina or Tahine—A paste made from ground sesame seeds and olive oil

Ta'leya—A garnish of onion and garlic fried in olive oil used in Egypt

Tamar—Date

Tamer Hind—Tamarind (literally means Indian date)

Tarama—The roe of red or grey mullet

Taratoor—Sauce or dip

Tareh—Garlic chives

Tatli Surubu—Sugar syrup

Tereyagli—Butter (Turkish)

Thawn or Tum—Garlic

Tiin—Fig. The fig is mentioned in the Bible and is a popular fruit in the Middle East. There are hundreds of varieties with skin colors of all hues. The flesh is usually blood-colored, with a multitude of seeds, and undoubtedly taste best fresh from the tree.

Tmar—Date

Turlu—Casserole using (usually) vegetables only (Turkish/Armenian)

W

Waraq il Ghar—Bay leaf

Warkah or Ouarka, Malsougva or Dioul—Tracing-paper-thin transparent pastry (Morocco)

Y

Yansoon—Aniseed

Yahni—Arab method of cooking. Meat or vegetables braised in oil with onion, then simmered with water to make a stock. Used from Egypt to Iran (and a derivative yakni, in India).

Yershig—Dried sausage (Armenian)

Z

Za'atar—A blend of powdered herbs, especially thyme with marjoram, sumak and (sometimes) roasted sesame seeds.

Za'faran—Saffron

Zanjabil—Ginger

Za'tar—Thyme

Zaytun, Zayt or Zeytun—Olive

Zeytunagli—Olive oil

Zereshk—Barberry, see Spice Glossary

Zhug—Spice mixture (Yemeni)

APPENDIX

Stock Items

Below are listed all the specialized ingredients used in this book. Items marked with an * are used in three or less recipes. The list may look formidable, but all these items will keep for a long time if stored correctly (best in airtight containers in a damp-free, dark place). And even if you need to buy everything the cost is relatively low. The items that are available by mail from The Curry Club are those which state quantities (see Appendix 1 for address). The quantities are either metric or imperial depending on the manufacturers.

Whole spices

Allspice 30 g
*Aniseed 45 g
*Barberry (zereshk) 25 g
Bay leaf 3 g
Cardamom, green 30 g
*Caraway 30 g
*Cassia bark 30 g
Cinnamon quill 20 g
Cloves 20 g
*Coriander seeds 45 g
*Cumin, black 25 g
Cumin, white 60 g
Fennel seed 25 g
*Fenugreek leaf 18 g
Fenugreek seed 40 g

*Mahlab 20 g
Mint, dried 40 g
*Mustard seed, black 60 g
Nutmeg 30 g
*Pomegranate seed 30 g
*Poppy seed, white 50 g
Saffron 0.5 g
Sesame seed, white 50 g
Thyme, dry 40 g
Turmeric 100 g
*Zereshk 25 g

Ground spices

*Cassia bark 25 g
Cayenne 100 g
Cinnamon 25 g
*Clove 25 g
Cumin, white 100 g
*Garlic powder 100 g
*Ginger powder 100 g
Paprika 100 g
Pepper, black 100 g
Pepper, white 100 g
*Sumak 65 g
Turmeric 100 g

182

Spice mixtures
Aromatic salt 100 g
Baharat 20 g
*Curry powder, mild 20 g
Gormeh sabzi 2 oz
Kookoo sabzi 2 oz
*La kama 20 g
Lebanese mixture 20 g
*Ras-el-hanout 30 g
*Za_atar 65 g
*Zhug 25 g

Nuts
Almonds, ground
Almonds, whole
Hazelnuts
Pine nuts 100 g
Pistachio 50 g
Walnut

Dry foods
*Apricot
Chickpeas 500 g
Couscous 500 g
Fava (ful medames) beans 500 g
Ful nabed 500 g
*Loomi (lime) 2 oz
Masoor dhal 500 g
*Melokhia (Egyptian leaves) 2 oz
Sultanas

Flours
All-purpose
Chapatti, brown 500 g
Corn flour
Strong white
Whole-wheat

Oils
Hazelnut
Olive
Sesame
Soy
Sunflower
Vegetable
Walnut
Smen (clarified butter) 200 g

Canned foods
Chickpeas 14 oz
Fava (ful medames) beans 14 oz
Harissa hot sauce 140 g
*Haricot white beans

Other items
Filo pastry
Lemon juice, bottled
*Milk powder
Orange-blossom water 50 ml
*Red food coloring, dry 25 g
Rice, basmati 2 kg
Rose water 50 ml
Sea salt
Sesame paste (tahini) 100 g
*Vine leaves
Wheat, cracked (bulgur) 500 g
*Wheat, whole

INDEX

OTHER COOKBOOKS BY THE CROSSING PRESS

Homestyle Cooking Series

Homestyle Mexican Cooking
By Lourdes Nichols
$16.95 • Paper • ISBN 0-89594-861-3

Homestyle Thai and Indonesian Cooking
By Sri Owen
$16.95 • Paper • ISBN 0-89594-859-1

Homestyle Italian Cooking
By Lori Carangelo
$16.95 • Paper • ISBN 0-89594-867-2

Global Cuisine

Global Grilling
Sizzling Recipes from Around the World
By Jay Solomon
$10.95 • Paper • ISBN 0-89594-666-1

Global Kitchen
*Meat and Vegetarian Recipes from Africa,
Asia and Latin America for Western Kitchens*
By Troth Wells
$16.95 • Paper • ISBN 0-89594-753-6

The World in Your Kitchen
*Vegetarian Recipes from Africa,
Asia and Latin America*
By Troth Wells
Foreword by Glenda Jackson
$16.95 • Paper • ISBN 0-89594-577-0

OTHER COOKBOOKS BY THE CROSSING PRESS

International Vegetarian Cooking
by Judy Ridgway
$14.95 • Paper • ISBN 0-89594-854-0

Island Cooking
Recipes from the Caribbean
By Dunstan Harris
$10.95 • Paper • ISBN 0-89594-400-6

Japanese Vegetarian Cooking
From Simple Soups to Sushi
By Patricia Richfield
$14.95 • Paper • ISBN 0-89594-805-2

Indian Cuisine

From Bengal to Punjab
The Cuisines of India
By Smita Chandra
$12.95 • Paper • ISBN 0-89594-509-6

The Spice Box
Vegetarian Indian Cookbook
By Manju Shivraj Singh
$12.95 • Paper • ISBN 0-89594-053-1

Taste of the Tropics
Traditional and Innovative Cooking from the Pacific and Caribbean
By Jay Solomon
$10.95 • Paper • ISBN 0-89594-533-9

Traveling Jamaica with Knife, Fork & Spoon
By Robb Walsh and Jay McCarthy
$16.95 • Paper • ISBN 0-89594-698-X

Identification of photographs following page 96:

Photo A: Salted Fish Roe Dip *(Taramasalata)* page 33, Fried Squid *(Mantiq Mehammer)* page 47, Chickpea and Sesame Dip *(Hummus B'Tahini)* page 32, Avocado Dip *(Sabra Dip)* page 35, Tabouli page 42, Chile Purée *(Harissa)* page 37, Greek Turkish Oval Bread *(Pita)*, page 146.

Photo B: Pigeon Pie *(Bisteeya)* page 58, Spinach with Feta Cheese Pie *(Spanokopitta)* page 60, with its filling in the small bowl below, Puff Pastry Pot *(Pastelles)* page 62, with mince and rice fillings below, Small Stuffed Pastries *(Boreks)* page 55, Tiny Arab Pizzas with Quail's Eggs *(S'finah)* page 63, and above them seafood and vegetable fillings.

Photo C: Ground Meat in a Kibbeh Shell *(Kibbeyets)* page 69, Iranian Bread *(Barbari)* page 147, Veal with Apricots *(Mishmisheya)* page 78, Miniature Meatballs *(Lahma-Kafta Bil Karaz)* page 67, Rice Crust *(Tahdig)* page 140, Roast Rabbit *(Arnhah Chermoula)* page 80, Rice with Dates *(Riz El Tammar)* page 142.

Photo D: Stuffed Quail *(Siman Bil Kibbeh)* page 92, Chicken with Dates and Honey *(Tagine Djej Bil Tamar Wa Assal)* page 89, Couscous-Stuffed Roast Chicken with Red Sauce in the accompanying jug *(Djej M'ahmar)* page 85, Circassian Chicken *(Cerkez Tavagu)* page 91, Plain Couscous, page 133.

Photo E: Arab Bread *(Khoubiz)* page 145, Baked Lobster *(Istakoz Firinda)* page 104, Spicy Fried Shrimps *(Nachbous)* page 100, with Iranian Rice *(Chellow)* page 139, Baked Curried Sea Trout *(Masgouf Baghdadi)* page 106, Skewered Swordfish *(Kilich Shish)* page 97, with its garlic dip.

Photo F: Vinegared Chiles *(Biber Tursu)* page 29, Herbal Omelette *(Kookoo Sabzi)* page 130, Yemeni Spicy Bread *(Saluf bi Hilbeh)* page 146, Chickpeas with Spinach *(Houmous ye Esfenaj)* page 123, Stir-Fried Okra *(Bamiya B'zayt)* page 116, Shredded Potato Cakes *(Latkes)* page 111, Pickled Lemon *(Limoon Makbous)* page 30, Pickles *(Torshi)* page 28, Stuffed Vine Leaves *(Dolmades)* page 125.

Photo G: Sweet Crisp Pastries *(Baklava)* page 153, Almond Snake Cake *(El M'Hancha)* page 156, Sweet, Crisp, Shredded Pastries *(Kadayif)* page 155, Syrupy Pancakes *(Ataif)* page 160, Fried Semolina Pudding *(Irmik Helvasi)* page 158.

Photo H: Sugared Almonds *(Lose Hiloo)* page 164, Stuffed Dates *(Sephardi Tamar)* page 162, Arab Coffee *(Q'Ahwah Arabiya)* page 167, Turkish Delight *(Rahat Lokum)* page 163, Moroccan Mint Tea *(Chai Bi Na'na)* page 169.

To receive a current catalog from
The Crossing Press
please call toll-free,
800-777-1048.